The Wine Explorer's Guide to

France

Hugh Baker

Wine Explorer's Guide Ltd

The Wine Explorer's Guide to France

Published by Wine Explorer's Guide Ltd
74 Wycliffe Road, London SW11 5QR

ISBN 0-9544205-0-0

Printed & bound in England by Millnet, London   www.millnet.co.uk

All profits from the sale of the first printing of this book will be donated to
The Foundation for the Study of Infant Deaths.

For Penny
my beloved wife and co-conspirator

Acknowledgements

First of all, thank you for buying this book and thereby supporting a charity whose work Penny and I have a close personal interest in. My sincerest thanks also go to all those who have given me such enthusiastic support and encouragement during this project, often accompanied by extensive practical testing! In particular, I would like to thank Charlie and Sandra, whose wedding and infectious enthusiasm triggered the whole idea. Many other friends need thanks, especially: Jake and Bex for editorial level-headedness; Jim for zany ideas on where this could go; Ana and Paul for numerous creative touches; Simon and Kourtney for inspirational feedback; Jonathan the design guru. I must also thank the partners and staff of Booz Allen Hamilton whose moral support and generosity have made the project viable, and the staff of the Battersea branches of Oddbins for their curiosity about early drafts. Finally, thanks to André and all at Millnet printers for their sympathy and support for the whole project.

Contents

Foreword

The purpose behind this book is simple: to encourage the exploration of French wines by demystifying the French wine classification system.

The French make more wine than any other country in the world, but 2001 was the first year that drinkers in the UK spent more on Australian wine than French wine. One reason for this is that the Australians and other New World wine producers discovered that the most easily recognisable characteristic of a wine is the grape variety, which they display prominently on their labels. By contrast, the French classify their wines by where they come from rather than what is in them. They call this the *appellation* system, and it was created because they believe that wine is the expression of its *terroir* (location, climate and soil), and over the centuries they have selected the perfect grape varieties for each place. However, consumers are voting with their wallets, and as a consequence are losing out on many wonderful French wines purely because it is not easy to find out what is in them.

The first section of this book is an overview of the wine making regions, which includes a map and a generalisation of the grape varieties used in each region. The second section is the main part of the book, and it goes through each region and each wine type (red, white, rosé and sparkling), grouping the appellations of that region by their primary grape varieties and graphically describing the style. For Bordeaux and Burgundy, this section also gives details of the hierarchy of appellations. The third section is an index of appellations, showing where they may be found in the second section. Finally, the fourth section is an index of all the grape varieties used, listing the appellations that include the grape variety as a pure varietal, primary variety, or secondary blending variety.

I have designed this book to lower the risk of trying new wines. For example, if you like white Sancerre a quick look in the index of appellations points you to page 37 covering the white wines of the Loire. This shows you that Sancerre is pure sauvignon blanc, and since you like Sancerre you would probably also like Menetou-Salon, Quincy, Reuilly, Pouilly-Fumé or Coteaux de Giennois, because they too are pure sauvignon blanc from the same "Central Vinyards" part of the Loire valley.

The appellation system has four levels. This book concentrates only on the highest level: the Appellations d'Origine Controlées wines, or AOC wines. These represent 52% of total French non-distilled wine output. The next level is Vins Délimités de Qualité Supérieure, or VDQS, which are less than 1% of total production and consequently harder to find. Then there is Vins de Pays (29%), and finally Vins de Table (18%). Vins de Pays are allowed to display the grape variety on their labels, thereby simplifying their selection. However, Vins de Table are not allowed to indicate grape variety or place of origin, so it is impossible to guess what grape varieties they contain.

I hope you enjoy the book, and happy exploring!

HTB

Section I:
French Wine Making Regions

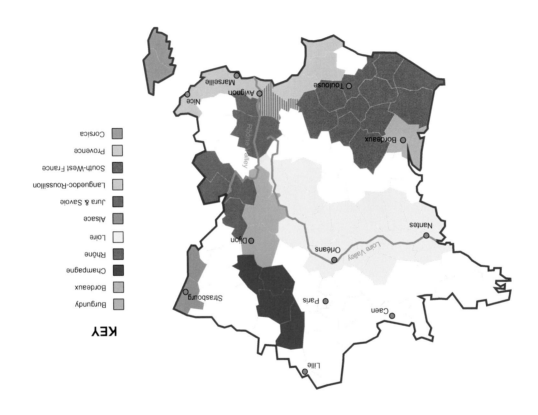

French Wine Making Regions

KEY

- Burgundy
- Bordeaux
- Champagne
- Rhône
- Loire
- Alsace
- Jura & Savoie
- Languedoc-Roussillon
- South-West France
- Provence
- Corsica

Lille

Paris

Strasbourg

Caen

Dijon

Nantes

Orléans

Loire Valley

Rhône Valley

Bordeaux

Toulouse

Nice

Marseille

Avignon

Primary Grape Varieties by Region

	Red & Rosé	White	Sparkling		Red & Rosé	White	Sparkling
Burgundy	Pinot Noir Gamay	Chardonnay Aligoté	Pinot Noir Pinot Gris Pinot Blanc Chardonnay	**Jura & Savoie**	Trousseau Poulsard Noir Pinot Noir Gamay	Chasselas Altesse Savagnin Chardonnay	Chasselas Altesse Savagnin Chardonnay
Bordeaux	Cabernet Savignon Cabernet Franc Merlot	Sémillon Sauvignon Blanc	Sémillon Sauvignon Blanc	**Languedoc-Roussillon**	Grenache Noir Carignan Cinsault	Grenache Blanc Clairette Muscat	Mauzac
Champagne	Chardonnay Pinot Noir Pinot Meunier	Chardonnay Pinot Noir Pinot Meunier	Chardonnay Pinot Noir Pinot Meunier	**South-West France**	Fer Servadou Tannat Négrette Malbec *Bordeaux blends*	Manseng Courbu *Bordeaux blends*	Len de l'El Sauvignon Blanc
Rhône	Grenache Noir Syrah	Marsanne Roussanne Viognier	Clairette Marsanne Roussanne Muscat	**Provence**	Mourvèdre Carignan Grenache Noir Cinsault	Clairette Ugni Blanc	-
Loire	Pinot Noir Cabernet Savignon Cabernet Franc Gamay	Chenin Blanc Sauvignon Blanc Melon de Bourgogne	Chenin Blanc	**Corsica**	Sciacarello Nielluccio	Vermentino Muscat	-
Alsace	Pinot Noir	Gewürztraminer Muscat Pinot Gris Riesling	Pinot Noir Pinot Gris Pinot Blanc Chardonnay				

Section II:
Appellations at a Glance

Primary Red Wine Appellations of Burgundy (1/2)

Pinot Noir blended with Pinot Gris and Pinot Liébault

KEY

- ■ Full-bodied
- ■ Medium-bodied
- ■ Light-bodied

Côtes de Beaune

- Pommard (Premier Cru) AOC
- Blagny (Côtes de Beaune)(P. Cru) AOC
- Monthelie (Côtes de Beaune) (P. Cru) AOC
- Meursault-Santenots AOC
- Volnay-Santenots Premier Cru AOC
- Meursault (Côtes de Beaune) (P. Cru) AOC
- Pernand-Vergelesses (Côtes de B.)(P. Cru) AOC
- Volnay (Premier Cru) AOC
- Savigny (-Lès-Beaune) (Côtes de B.)(P. Cru) AOC
- St.-Romain (Côtes de Beaune) AOC
- Santenay (Côtes de Beaune)(P. Cru) AOC
- St.-Aubin (Côtes de Beaune)(P. Cru) AOC

- Maranges (Côtes de Beaune) (P. Cru) AOC
- Chassagne-Montrachet (Côtes de B.)(P. Cru) AOC
- Puligny-Montrachet (Côtes de B.)(P. Cru) AOC
- Ladoix (Côtes de Beaune) (Premier Cru) AOC
- Chorey-Lès-Beaune (Côtes de Beaune) AOC
- Auxey-Duresses (Côtes de Beaune)(P. Cru) AOC
- (Le) Corton Grand Cru AOC
- Aloxe-Corton (Premier Cru) AOC
- Côtes de Beaune Villages AOC
- Côtes de Beaune AOC
- Bourgogne Haute-Côtes de Beaune AOC
- Beaune (Premier Cru) AOC

Côtes de Nuits

- Bourgogne Hautes-Côtes de Nuits AOC
- Grand Echézeaux Grand Cru AOC
- Echézeaux Grand Cru AOC
- Latricières-Chambertin Grand Cru AOC
- Griottes-Chambertin Grand Cru AOC
- Chambertin Grand Cru AOC
- Ruchottes-Chambertin Grand Cru AOC
- Mazy-Chambertin/Mazis Grand Cru AOC
- Mazoyères-Chambertin Grand Cru AOC
- Charmes-Chambertin Grand Cru AOC
- Chambertin-Clos de Bèze Grand Cru AOC
- Chapelle-Chambertin Grand Cru AOC
- Gevrey-Chambertin (Premier Cru) AOC

- Nuits (-St.-Georges) (Premier Cru) AOC
- Clos de Tart Grand Cru AOC
- Clos St.-Denis Grand Cru AOC
- Clos de la Roche Grand Cru AOC
- Clos du Lambrays Grand Cru AOC
- Morey-St.-Denis (Premier Cru) AOC
- La Tâche Grand Cru AOC
- Romanée-Conti Grand Cru AOC
- La Romanée Grand Cru AOC
- Richebourg Grand Cru AOC
- La Grand Rue Grand Cru AOC
- Romanée-St.-Vivant Grand Cru AOC
- Vosne-Romanée (Premier Cru) AOC

- Fixin (Premier Cru) AOC
- Musigny Grand Cru AOC
- Bonnes Mares Grand Cru AOC
- Chambolle-Musigny (Premier Cru) AOC
- Marsannay (La Côte) AOC
- Côtes Nuits-Villages AOC
- Clos de Vougeot Grand Cru AOC
- Vougeot (Premier Cru) AOC

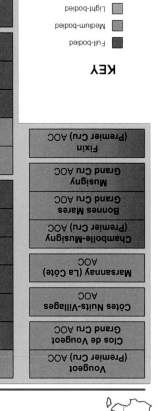

Pinot Noir and Gamay

Bourgogne Passetoutgrains AOC

Pinot Noir with up to 33% Gamay and 15% Chardonnay, Pinot Blanc and Pinot Gris

Pinot Noir blended with Pinot Gris and Pinot Liébault

Bourgogne AOC

May also contain César, Tressot, Gamay

Bourgogne Grand-Ordinaire AOC

Bourgogne (village name) AOC

May also contain César, Tressot

Generic Burgundy

Givry (Premier Cru) AOC

Rully (Premier Cru) AOC

Mercurey (Premier Cru) AOC

Côte Chalonnaise

Gamay blended with Pinot Noir and Pinot Gris

Beaujolais (village name) AOC

Beaujolais Supérieur AOC

Beaujolais-Villages AOC

Côtes de Brouilly AOC (Cru Beaujolais)

Beaujolais

Mâcon AOC

Mâcon (village name) AOC

Mâcon Supérieur AOC

Mâconnais

Gamay

Brouilly AOC (Cru Beaujolais)

May also contain Chardonnay, Aligoté, Melon de Bourgogne

Chiroubles AOC (Cru Beaujolais)

Coteaux du Lyonnais AOC (Cru Beaujolais)

Régnié AOC (Cru Beaujolais)

Fleurie AOC (Cru Beaujolais)

Juliénas AOC (Cru Beaujolais)

St.-Amour AOC (Cru Beaujolais)

Chénas AOC (Cru Beaujolais)

Morgon AOC (Cru Beaujolais)

Moulin-à-Vent AOC (Cru Beaujolais)

KEY

- Full-bodied
- Medium-bodied
- Light-bodied

Côtes de Beaune

Grands Crus

Corton

Premiers Crus

Aloxe-Corton Premier Cru

Auxey-Duresses (Côtes de Beaune) Premier Cru
Beaune Premier Cru
Blagny (Côtes de Beaune) Premier Cru
Chassagne-Montrachet (Côtes de Beaune) Premier Cru
Ladoix (Côtes de Beaune) Premier Cru
Maranges(Côtes de Beaune) Premier Cru
Monthelie (Côtes de Beaune) Premier Cru

Pernand-Vergelesses (Côtes de Beaune) Premier Cru
Pommard Premier Cru
Puligny-Montrachet (Côtes de Beaune) Premier Cru
St.-Aubin (Côtes de Beaune) Premier Cru
Santenay (Côtes de Beaune) Premier Cru
Savigny (-Lès-Beaune)(Côtes de Beaune) Premier Cru
Volnay Premier Cru

Meursault
(Côtes de Beaune)
Premier Cru
Volnay-Santenots
Premier Cru
Meursault-
Santenots

Village Wines

Aloxe-Corton

Auxey-Duresses (Côtes de Beaune)
Beaune
Blagny (Côtes de Beaune)
Chassagne-Montrachet (Côtes de Beaune)
Ladoix (Côtes de Beaune)
Maranges (Côtes de Beaune)
Monthelie (Côtes de Beaune)

Pernand-Vergelesses (Côtes de Beaune)
Pommard
Puligny-Montrachet (Côtes de Beaune)
St.-Aubin (Côtes de Beaune)
Santenay (Côtes de Beaune)
Savigny (-Lès-Beaune)(Côtes de Beaune)
Volnay

Meursault
(Côtes de Beaune)

Bourgogne Haute-
Côtes de Beaune
Côtes de Beaune
Côtes de Beaune-
Villages
Chorey-Lès-Beaune
(Côtes de Beaune)
St.-Romain
(Côtes de Beaune)

Bourgogne Grand-Ordinaire / Bourgogne Passetoutgrains AOC

Basic

Bourgogne / Bourgogne <Village Name>

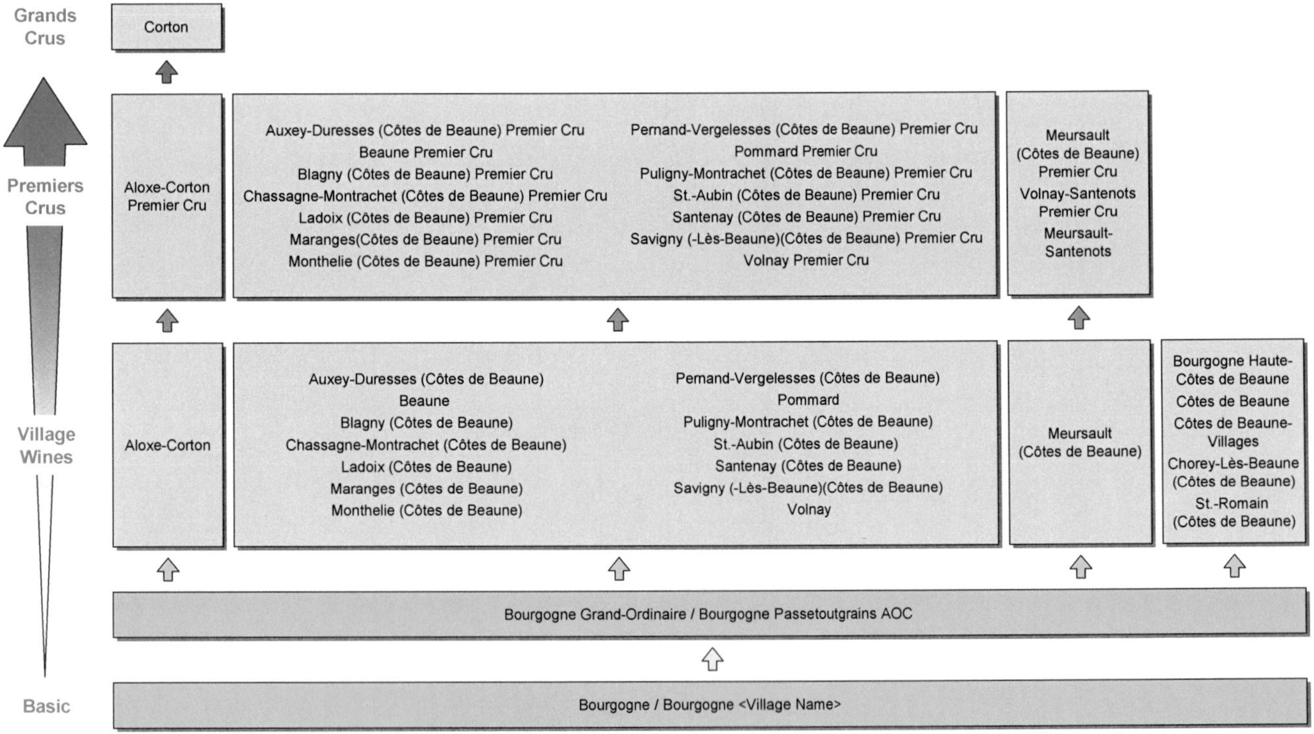

Red Wine Appellation Hierarchy of Burgundy (2/2)

Côte Chalonnaise

Côtes de Nuits

Beaujolais

Grands Crus

| Echézeaux Grand Echézeaux | Romanée-St.-Vivant La Grand Rue Richebourg La Romanée Romanée-Conti La Tâche | Clos Vougeot | Bonnes Mares Musigny | Clos du Lambrays Clos de la Roche Clos St.-Denis Clos de Tart | Chapelle-Chambertin Chambertin-Clos de Bèze Charmes-Chambertin Mazoyères-Chambertin Mazy-Chambertin/Mazis Ruchottes-Chambertin Chambertin Griottes-Chambertin Latricères-Chambertin |

Premiers Crus

| Givry Premier Cru Mercurey Premier Cru Rully Premier Cru | Flagey-Echézeaux | Vosne-Romanée Premier Cru | Vougeot Premier Cru | Chambolle-Musigny Premier Cru | Morey-St.-Denis Premier Cru | Gevrey-Chambertin Premier Cru | Nuits (-St.-Georges) Premier Cru Fixin Premier Cru | Côtes de Brouilly Brouilly Chiroubles Coteaux de Lyonnais Régnié Fleurie Juliénas St.-Amour Chénas Morgon Moulin-à-Vent |

Village Wines

| Givry Mercurey Rully | | Vosne-Romanée | Vougeot | Chambolle-Musigny | Morey-St.-Denis | Gevrey-Chambertin | Nuits (-St.-Georges) Fixin | Marsannay (La Côte) Bourgogne Hautes-Côtes de Nuits Côtes Nuits-Villages |

Bourgogne Grand-Ordinaire / Bourgogne Passetoutgrains AOC

Beaujolais Supérieur

Basic

Bourgogne / Bourgogne <Village Name>

Beaujolais <Village Name>

Côtes de Beaune

Aloxe-Corton

Les Chaillots, La Coutière, Les Fournières, Les Guérets, La Maréchaude, Clos des Maréchaudes, Les Maréchaudes, Les Meix/Clos du Chapitre, Les Moutottes, Les Paulands, Les Petites Lolières, La Toppe au Vert, Les Valozières, Les Vercots

Auxey-Duresses

Bas des Duresses, Les Bretterins, La Chapelle, Climat du Val, Les Duresses, Les Écusseaux, Les Grands-Champs, Reugne

Beaune

Les Aigrots, Aux Coucherias/Clos de la Féguine, Aux Cras, Clos des Avaux, Les Avaux, Le Bas de Teurons, Les Beaux Fougets, Belissand, Les Blanches Fleurs, Les Champs Pimont, Les Chouacheux, l'Écu/Clos de l'Écu, Les Epenottes/Les Epenotes, Les Fèves, En Genêt, Les Grèves, Clos Landry/Clos Ste.-Landry, Les Longes, Le Clos des Mouches, Clos de la Mousse, Les Marconnets, Le Mignotte, Montée Rouge, Les Montrevenots, En l'Orme, Les Perrières, Pertuisots, Les Reversées, Clos du Roi, Les Seurey, Les Sizies, Clos Ste.-Anne/Sur les Grèves, Les Teurons, Les Toussaints, Les Tuvilains, Le Vigne de l'Enfant Jésus, Les Vignes Franches/Clos des Ursules

Blagny

La Garenne/Sur la Garenne, Hameau de Blagny, La Jeunelotte, La Pièce sous le Bois, Sous Blagny, Sous le Dos d'Ane, Sous le Puits

Chassagne-Montrachet

Abbaye de Morgeot, Les Baudines, Blanchot Dessus, Les Boirettes, Bois de Chassagne, Les Bondues, La Boudriotte, Les Brussonnes, En Cailleret, La Cardeuse, Champ Jendreau, Les Champs Gain, La Chapelle, Clos Chareau, Les Chaumées, Les Chaumes, Les Chenevottes, Les Combards, Les Commes, Ez Crets, Ez Crottes, Dent de Chien, Les Embrazées, Les Fairendes, Francemont, Le Grande Borne, La Grande Montagne, Les Grandes Ruchottes, Les Grand Clos, Guerchère, Les Macherelles, La Maltroie, Les Morgeots, Les Murées, Les Pasquelles, Petingeret, Les Petites Fairendes, Les Petits Clos, Les Places, Les Rebichets, En Remilly, La Romanée, La Roquemaure, Clos St.-Jean, Tête du Clos, Tonton Marcel, Les Vergers, Vide Bourse, Vigne Blanche, Vigne Derrière, En Virondot

Ladoix

Basses Mourottes, Bois Roussot, Les Buis, Le Clou d'Orge, La Corvée, Les Gréchons, Hautes Mourottes, Les Joyeuses, La Micaude, En Naget, Rognet et Corton

Maranges

Clos de la Boutière, La Croix Moines, La Fussière, Le Clos des Loyères, Le Clos des Rois, Les Clos Roussots

Meursault

Aux Perrières, Les Bouchères, Les Caillerets, Les Charmes-Dessous/Les Charmes-Dessus, Les Chaumes de Narvaux, Les Chaumes de Perrières, Les Cras, Les Genevrières-Dessous/Les Genevrières-Dessus, Les Gouttes d'Or, La Jeunelotte, Clos des Perrières, Les Perrières-Dessous/Les Perrières-Dessus, La Pièce sous le Bois, Les Plures, Le Porusot, Les Porusot-Dessous/Les Porusot-Dessus, Clos des Richemont/Cras, Les Santenots Blancs, Les Santenots du Milieu*, Sous Blagny, Sous le Dos d'Ane

*Note * red wines from Les Santenots du Milieu may also be labelled Volnay-Santenots Premier Cru AOC*

Monthelie

La Cas Rougeot, Les Champs Fuillot, Les Duresses, La Château Gaillard, Le Clos Gauthey, Le Meix Bataille, Les Riottes, Sur la Velle, La Taupine, Les Vignes Rondes, Le Village do Monthelie

Pernand Vergelesses

En Caradeux, Creux de la Net, Les Fichots, Île des Hautes Vergelesses, Les Basses Vergelesses

Pommard

Les Arvelets, Les Bertins, Clos Blanc, Les Boucherottes, La Chanière, Les Chanlins-Bas, Les Chaponnières, Les Charmots, Les Combes-Dessus, Clos de la Commaraine, Les Croix Noires, Derrière St.-Jean, Clos des Epeneaux, Les Fremiers, Les Grands Epenots, Les Jarolières, En Largillière/Les Argillières, Clos Micot, Les Petits Epenots, Les Pézerolles, La Platière, Les Poutures, La Refène, Les Rugiens-Bas, Les Rugiens-Hauts, Les Saussilles, Clos de Verger, Village

St.-Aubin

La Bas de Gamay à l'Est, Bas de Vermarain à l'Est, Les Castets, Les Cahmplots, En Champs, Le Charmois, La Chatenière, Les Combes au Sud, Les Cortons, En Créot, Derrière chez Edouard, Derrière la Tour, Echaille, Les Frionnes, Sur Gamay, Marinot, En Montceau, Les Murgers des Dents de Chien, Les Perrières, Pitangeret, Le Puits, En la Ranché, En Remilly, Sous Roche Dumay, Sur le Sentier du Clou, Les Travers de Marinot, Vignes Moingeon, Le Village, En Vollon à l'Est

Santenay

Beauregard, Le Chainey, La Comme, Comme Dessus, Clos Faubard, Les Fourneaux, Grand Clos Rousseau, Les Gravières, La Maladière, Clos de Mouches, Passetemps, Petit Clos Rousseau, Clos de Tavannes

Savigny-Lès-Beaune

Aux Clous, Aux Fournaux, Aux Gravains, Aux Guettes, Aux Serpentières, Bas Marconnets, Basses Vergelesses, Clos la Bataillères/Les Vergelesses, Champ Chevrey/Aux Fournaux, Les Chamières, Hauts Jarrons/La Dominodes, Les Lavières, Les Narbantons, Petits Godeaux, Les Peuillets, Redrescut, Les Rouvrettes, Les Talmettes

Volnay

Les Angles, Les Aussy, La Barre, (Clos de la) Bousse d'Or, Les Brouillards, En Cailleret, Les Cailleret, Cailleret Dessus/Clos des 60 Ouvrées, Carelles Dessous, Dacrelle sous la Chapelle, Clos de la Caves de Ducs, En Champans, Chanlin, En Chevret, Clos de la Chapelle, Clos de Chênes/Clos de Chânes, Clos de Ducs, Clos du Château des Ducs, Frèmiets/Clos de la Rougeotte, La Gigotte, Les Grands Champs, Lassolle, Les Lurets, Les Mitans, En l'Ormeau, Pitures Dessus, Pointes d'Angles, Robardelle, Le Ronceret, Taille Pieds, En Verseuil/Clos du Verseuil, Le Village

Côtes de Nuits

Chambolle-Musigny

Les Amoureuses, Les Baudes, Aux Chabiots, Les Charmes, Les Châtelots, La Combe d'Orveau, Aux Combottes, Les Combottes, Les Feusselottes, Les Fuées, Les Grand Murs, Les Groseilles, Les Gruenchers, Les Haut Doix, Les Lavrottes, Les Noirots, Les Plantes, Les Sentiers

Gevrey-Chambertin

Bel Air, La Bossière, Les Cazetiers, Champeaux, Champitennois, Champonnet, Clos du Chapitre, Cherbandes, Les Corbeaux, Craipillot, En Ergot, Etournelles/ Estournelles, Fonteny, Les Goulots, Lavaut/Lavout St.-Jacques, La Perrière, Petite Chapelle, Petits Cazetiers, Plantigone/Issarts, Poissenot, Clos Prieur-Haut/Clos Prieure, La Romanée, Le Clos St.-Jacques, Les Varoilles

Morey-St.-Denis

Clos Baulet, Les Blanchards, La Bussière, Les Chaffots, Aux Charmes, Les Charrières, Les Chénevery, Aux Cheseaux, Les Faconnières, Les Genevrières, Les Gruenchers, Les Millandes, Monts Luisants, Des Ormes, Clos Sorbè, Les Sorbès, Côte Rôtie, La Riotte, Les Ruchots, Le Village

Vougeot

Les Crâs, Clos de la Perrière, Les Petit Vougeots, La Vigne Blanche

Fixin

Les Arvelets, Clos du Chapitre, Clos de la Perrière (m), Aux Cheusots, Les Hervelets, Le Meix Bas, La Perrière, Queue de Hareng, En Suchot, Le Village

Nuits-St.-Georges

Les Argillats, Les Argillières, Clos Arlot, Aux Boudots, Aux Bousselots, Les Cailles, Les Chaboeufs, Aux Chaignots, Chaine-Carteau/Chaines-Carteaux, Aux Champs Perdrix, Clos des Corvées, Clos des Corvées Pagets, Aux Cras, Les Crots, Les Damodes, Les Didiers, Les Forêts/Clos des Forêts St.-Georges, Les Grandes Vignes, Château Gris, Les Hauts Pruliers, Clos de la Maréchale, Aux Murgers, Aux Perdrix, En la Perrière Noblet, Les Perrières, Les Porets, Les Poulettes, Les Procès, Les Pruliers, La Richemone, La Roncière, Rue de Chaux, Les St.-Georges, Clos St.-Marc/Aux Corvées, Les Terres Blanches, Aux Thorey, Les Vallerots, Les Vaucrains, Aux Vignerondes

Vosne-Romanée

Les Beaux Monts, Les Beaux Monts Bas, Les Beaux Monts Hauts, Les Brûlées, La Croix Rameau, Cros-Parantoux, Les Gaudichots, Les Hauts Beaux Monts, Aux Malconsorts, En Orveaux, Les Petits Monts, Clos des Réas, Aux Reignots, Les Rouges du Dessus, Les Suchots

Côte Chalonnaise

Givry

Clos de la Barraude, Les Berges, Bois Chevaux, Bois Gauthier, Clos de Cellier aux Moines, Clos Charlé, Clos du Cras Long, Les Grandes Vignes, Grands Prétants, Clos Jus, Clos Marceaux, Marole, Petit Marole, Petit Prétants, Clos St.-Paul, Clos St.-Pierre, Clos Salomon, Clos de la Servoisine, Vaux, Clos de Vernoy, En Vignes Rouge, Le Vigron

Mercurey

La Bondue, Les Byots, La Cailloute, Champs Martins, La Chassière, Le Clos, Clos des Barraults, Clos Château de Montaigu, Clos l'Evêque, Clos de Myglands, Clos du Roi, Les Tonnere, Clos Voyens/Les Voyens, Les Combins, Les Crêts, Les Criochots, Les Fourneaux/Clos des Fourneaux, Grand Clos Fortoul, Les Grands Voyens, Griffères, Le Levrière, Le Marcilly/Clos Marcilly, La Mission, Les Montaigus/Clos des Montaigus, Les Naugues, Les Petits Voyens, Les Ruelles, Sazenay, Les Vasées, Les Velley

Rully

Agneux, Bas de Vauvry, la Bressaude, Champ-Clou, Chapitre, Clos du Chaigne, Clos St.-Jacques, Cloux/Les Cloux, Ecloseaux, La Fosse, Grésigny, Margotey/Margoté, Marissou, Meix-Caillet, Mont-Palais, Moulesne/Molesme, Phillot, Les Pieres, Pillot, Préau, La Pucelle, Raboursay/Rabourcé, Raclot, La Renarde, Vauvry

Generic Burgundy

Bourgogne Villages

Côte de Beaune
La Chapelle Notre-Dame

Côtes de Nuits
La Chapitre, Montrecul/Montre-cul/En Montre-cul

Chablis
Côtes d'Auxerre, Chitry, Coulanges-la-Vineuse, Epineuil, Irancy, Saint-Bris, Côte St.-Jacques

Mâconnais

Mâcon Villages

Bissy, Braye, Davayé, Pierreclos

Beaujolais

Beaujolais Villages

Arbuisonnas, Les Ardillats, Beaujeu, Blacé, Chânes, Charentay, Chénas, Denicé, Durette, Lancié, Lantignié, Marchampt, Montmelas, Odenas, Le Perréon, Rivolet, St.Étiennes-des-Ouillères, St-Julien, St.-Lager, Salles, Vaux, Vauxrenard

Note: it is possible to find other village names under the Beaujolais (village name) AOC, but these others are allowed to use higher priced appellations including Cru Beaujolais, Mâcon-Villages AOC and St.-Veran AOC, so seldom use village Beaujolais

Red Wine Appellations of Bordeaux

Cabernet Sauvignon, Cabernet Franc and Merlot, blended with Malbec

Cabernet Sauvignon, Cabernet Franc and Merlot, blended with Malbec, Carmenère and Petit Verdot

St.-Émilion (classification) AOC

May also contain Carmenère

Lussac-St.-Émilion AOC

May also contain Carmenère

Montagne-St.-Émilion AOC

Puisseguin-St.-Émilion AOC

May also contain Carmenère

St.-Georges-St.-Émilion AOC

Pomerol AOC

Lalande-de-Pomerol AOC

Bordeaux-Côtes-de-Francs AOC

Bordeuax Supérieur Côtes-de-Francs AOC

Libournais

Margaux AOC

St.-Julien AOC

Pauillac AOC

St.-Estèphe AOC

Médoc AOC

Haut-Médoc AOC

Listrac-Médoc AOC

Moulis (-en-Médoc) AOC

Médoc

Côtes-de-Castillon AOC

Generic Bordeaux

Bordeaux AOC

Bordeaux Supérieur AOC

Côtes de Bourg AOC

Premières Côtes de Bourg AOC

Bourg

Graves AOC

May also contain Petit Verdot

Graves

Pessac-Léognan AOC

Premières Côtes de Bordeaux AOC

Graves de Vayres AOC

Ste.-Foy-Bordeaux AOC

Entre-Deux-Mers

Blaye/Blayais AOC

May also contain Prolongeau, Béguignol, Petit Verdot

Blaye

Côtes-Canon-Fronsac/ Canon-Fronsac AOC

Fronsac AOC

Fronsadais

KEY

Full-bodied

Medium-bodied

Light-bodied

Red Wine Appellation Hierarchy of Bordeaux

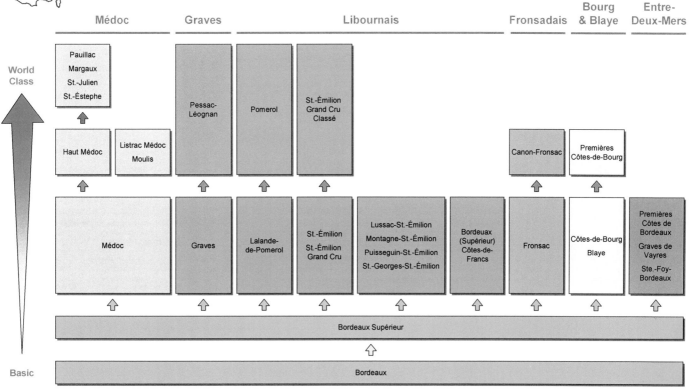

Médoc	Graves	Libournais	Fronsadais	Bourg & Blaye	Entre-Deux-Mers

World Class

| Pauillac / Margaux / St.-Julien / St.-Éstephe | | | | | |

| Haut Médoc | Listrac Médoc / Moulis | Pessac-Léognan | Pomerol | St.-Émilion Grand Cru Classé | | Canon-Fronsac | Premières Côtes-de-Bourg | |

| Médoc | Graves | Lalande-de-Pomerol | St.-Émilion / St.-Émilion Grand Cru | Lussac-St.-Émilion / Montagne-St.-Émilion / Puisseguin-St.-Émilion / St.-Georges-St.-Émilion | Bordeaux (Supérieur) Côtes-de-Francs | Fronsac | Côtes-de-Bourg / Blaye | Premières Côtes de Bordeaux / Graves de Vayres / Ste.-Foy-Bordeaux |

Bordeaux Supérieur

Basic

Bordeaux

Red Wine Producer Classifications of Bordeaux

Médoc

Pauillac

Premier Cru Classé
Château Lafite-Rothschild, Château Mouton-Rothschild, Château Latour

Second Cru Classé
Château Pichon-Longueville-Baron, Château Pichon-Longueville-Comtesse-de-Lalande

Quartrième Cru Classé
Château Duhart-Milon

Cinquième Cru Classé
Château Pontet-Conet, Château Batailley, Château Haut-Batailley, Château Grand-Puy-Lacoste, Château Lynch-Bages, Lynch-Moussas, Château d'Armailhac, Château Haut-Bages-Libéral, Château Pédesclaux, Château Clerc-Milon, Château Croizet-Bages

Margaux

Premier Cru Classé
Château Margaux

Second Cru Classé
Château Rauzan-Ségla, Château Rauzan-Gassies, Château Durfort-Vivens, Château Lascombes, Château Brane-Cantenac

Troisième Cru Classé
Château Kirwan, Château d'Issan, Château Giscours, Château Malescot-St.-Exupéry, Château Boyd-Cantenac, Château Cantenac-Brown, Château Palmer, Château Desmirail, Château Ferrière, Château Marquis d'Alesme-Becker

Quartrième Cru Classé
Château Pouget, Château Prieuré-Lichine, Château Marquis-de-Terme

Cinquième Cru Classé
Château Dauzac, Château Du Tertre

St.Julien

Second Cru Classé
Château Léoville-Las-Cases, Château Léoville-Poyferré, Château Léoville-Barton, Château Gruaud-Larose, Château Ducru-Beaucaillou

Troisième Cru Classé
Château Lagrange, Château Langoa-Barton

Quartrième Cru Classé
Château St.-Pierre-Sevaistre, Talbot, Château Branaire-Ducru, Château Beychevelle

St.-Estèphe

Second Cru Classé
Château Cos d'Estournel, Château Montrose

Troisième Cru Classé
Château Calon-Ségur

Quartrième Cru Classé
Château Lafon-Rochet

Cinquième Cru Classé
Château Cos Labory

Haut-Médoc

Troisième Cru Classé
Château La Lagune

Quartrième Cru Classé
Château La Tour-Carnet

Cinquième Cru Classé
Château Belgrave, Château Camensac, Château Centemerle

Libournais

St.-Emilion

Premier Grand Cru Classé and Grand Cru Classé wines may append their classification to St.-Emilion AOC on their labels. Note that St.-Emilion Grand Cru (but not classé) AOC wines are merely slightly superior than plain St.-Emilion AOC in requiring lower yields and higher alcohol, and are not château-specific.

Premier Grand Cru Classé, Class A
Ch. Ausone, Ch. Cheval Blanc

Premier Grand Cru Classé, Class B
Ch. l'Angelus, Ch. Beau-Séjour Bécot, Ch. Beauséjour, Ch. Belair, Ch. Canon, Ch.-Figeac, Clos Fourtet, Ch. la Gaffelière, Ch. Magdelaine, Ch. Pavie, Ch. Trottevielle

Grand Cru Classé
Ch. l'Arrosée, Ch. Côte de Baleau, Ch. Balestard la Tonnelle, Ch. Bellevue, Ch. Bergat, Ch. Berlinquet, Ch. Cadet-Bon, Ch. Cadet-Piola, Ch. Canon-la- Gaffelière, Ch. Cap de Mourlin, Ch. de Châtelet, Ch. Chauvin, Ch. Clos des Jacobins, Ch. la Clotte, Ch. la Clusière, Ch. Corbin, Ch. Corbin Michotte, Ch. la Couspaude, Ch. Coutet, Couvent des Jacobins, Ch. Croque Michotte, Ch. Curé Bon de la Madeleine, Ch. Dassault, Ch. la Dominique, Ch. Faurie de Souchard, Ch. Fonplégade, Ch. Fonroque, Ch. Franc-Mayne, Ch. Grand Barrail Lamarzelle Figeac, Ch. Grand Corbin, Ch. Grand-Corbin-Despagne, Ch. Grand Mayne, Ch. Grandes Murailles, Ch. Grand-Pontet, Ch. Guadet-Pontet, Ch. Haut-Corbin, Ch. Haut-Sarpe, Ch. Jean Faure, Ch. Laniote, Ch. Larcis Ducasse, Ch. Larmande, Ch. Laroque, Ch. Laroze, Clos la Madeleine, Ch. Lamarzelle, Ch. Matras, Ch. Mauvezin, Ch. Moulin du Cadet, Clos de l'Oratoire, Ch. Pavie Décesse, Ch. Pavie Macquin, Ch. Pavillion-Cadet, Ch. Petit-Faurie-de-Soutard, Ch. Le Prieuré, Ch. Ripeau, Ch. St.-Georges (Côte Pavie), Clos St.-Martin, Ch. Sansonnet, Ch. le Serre, Ch. Soutard, Ch. Tertre Daugay, Ch. la Tour Figeac, Ch. la Tour du Pin Figeac, Ch. Trimoulet, Ch. Troplong-Mondot, Ch. Villemaurine, Ch. Yon-Figeac

Pomerol

No formal classification system, however the following châteaux are world-renowned:

Château la Conseillante, Château l'Evangile, Château la Fleur Pétrus, Château Pétrus, Château Le Pin, Château Totanay

Graves

Pessac-Léognan

Premier Cru Classé
Château Haut-Brion

Cru Classé
Château Bouscaut, Château Carbonnieux, Domaine de Chevalier, Château de Fieuzal, Château Haut-Bailly, Château Malartic-Lagravière, Château La Mission-Haut-Brion, Château Olivier, Château Pape-Clément, Château Smith-Haut-Lafitte, Château La Tour Haut-Brion, Château La Tour-Martillac

Red Wine Appellations of the Rhône

Grenache Noir dominated blends

Côtes de Lubéron AOC

At least 60% Grenache Noir and Syrah, of which Syrah must be at least 10%, with maximum 40% Mourvèdre, maximum 20% Carignan, maximum 20% Cinsault and maximum 10% in total of Counoise, Pinot Noir, Gamay and Picpoul

Vacqueyras AOC

At least 50% Grenache Noir, up to 20% in total of Syrah, Mourvèdre, and Cinsault, and up to 10% in total of Terret Noir, Counoise, Muscardin, Vaccarèse, Gamay and Camarèse

Southern Rhône

KEY

- Full-bodied
- Medium-bodied
- Light-bodied
- Sweet Fortified

Côtes-du-Rhône-Villages AOC

May also maximum 65% Grenache Noir, at least 25% in total Syrah, Mourvèdre and Cinsault, and a maximum 10% in total of Clairette, Picpoul, Terret Noir, Picardan, Roussanne, Marsanne, Bourboulenc, Viognier, Carignan, and the standard Côtes-du-Rhône blending varieties *

Gigondas AOC

Up to 80% Grenache Noir, with at least 15% Syrah and Mourvèdre, maximum 20% Carignan, with up to 10% in total of Clairette, Picpoul, Terret Noir, Picardan, Cinsault, Roussanne, Marsanne, Bourboulenc, Viognier and the standard Côtes-du-Rhône blending varieties*

Lirac AOC

At least 40% Grenache Noir, at least 25% Syrah and Mourvèdre, and up to 10% of Carignan, and Cinsault

* Note: the standard red Côtes-du-Rhône blending varieties are: Counoise, Muscardin, Vaccarèse, Pinot Blanc, Mauzac, Pascal Blanc, Ugni Blanc, Calitor, Gamay and Camarèse

Grenache Noir, Syrah, Cinsault and Mourvèdre

Côtes-du-Rhône AOC

May also contain Picpoul, Terret Noir, Picardan, Roussanne, Bourboulenc, Viognier, maximum 30% Clairette, and a maximum 30% in total of the standard Côtes-du-Rhône blending varieties *

Châteauneuf-du-Pape AOC

May also contain Picpoul Noir, Terret Noir, Counoise, Muscardin, Vaccarèse, Picardan, Clairette, Roussanne and Bourboulenc

Coteaux du Tricastin AOC

May also contain Picpoul Noir, up to 20% Carignan, and up to 20% in total od Grenache Blanc, Clairette, Bourboulenc and Ugni Blanc

Coteaux de Pierrevert AOC

May also contain Carignan and Terret Noir

Côtes du Ventoux AOC

May also contain up to 30% Carignan, and a maximum 20% in total of Picpoul Noir, Counoise, Clairette, Bourboulenc, Grenache Blanc, Roussanne, Ugni Blanc, Picpoul Blanc and Pascal Blanc

Syrah

St.-Joseph AOC

May also contain up to 10% Marsanne and Roussanne

Cornas AOC

Côte Rôtie AOC

May also contain up to 20% Viognier

Crozes-Hermitage AOC

May also contain up to 15% Marsanne and Roussanne

(L') Hermitage AOC

May also contain up to 15% Marsanne and Roussanne

Brézème-Côtes-du-Rhône AOC (Syrah)

Usually varietal Syrah, up it is permitted to add some Marsanne or Rousanne

Gamay

Châtillon-en-Diois AOC

May also contain up to 25% Syrah and Pinot Noir

Northern Rhône

Grenache Blanc or Gris

Rasteau (Rancio) AOC

(Vin Doux Naturel) At least 90% Grenache (Gris or Blanc), with up to 10% in total of Clairette, Picpoul, Terret Noir, Picardan, Roussanne, Marsanne, Bourboulenc, Viognier and the other standard Côtes-du-Rhône blending varieties*

23

Red Wine Appellations of the Loire, Alsace & Champagne

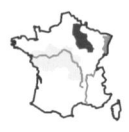

Pinot Noir

- **Menetou-Salon** AOC
- **Sancerre** AOC
- **Reuilly** AOC

May also contain Pinot Gris

Central Vinyards

- **(Vin d') Alsace** AOC (Pinot Noir)

Alsace

Cabernet Franc and Cabernet Sauvignon

- **Touraine-Amboise** AOC
  May also contain Malbec, Gamay
- **Touraine-Mesland** AOC
  May also contain Malbec, Gamay
- **Anjou-Villages** AOC
- **Saumur** AOC
  May also contain Pineau d'Aunis
- **Saumur-Champigny** AOC
  May also contain Pineau d'Aunis

Cabernet Franc

- **Chinon** AOC
  May also contain up to 10% Caberbet Savuignon
- **Bourgueil** AOC
  May also contain up to 10% Caberbet Savuignon
- **St.-Nicholas-de-Bourgueil** AOC
  May also contain up to 10% Caberbet Savuignon
- **Anjou** AOC
  May also contain Pineau d'Aunis

Gamay

- **Cheverny** AOC
  Between 40% and 65% Gamay, with Pinot Noir, Cabernet Franc and Malbec
- **Touraine** AOC
  Gamay blended with Cabernet Franc, may also contain Cabernet Sauvignon, Malbec, Pinot Noir, Pinot Meunier, Pinot Gris, Pineau d'Aunis
- **Anjou Gamay** AOC

Pineau d'Aunis

- **Coteaux de Loir** AOC
  At least 30% Pinot d'Aunis, may also contain Gamay, Pinot Noir, Cabernet Franc, Cabernet Sauvignon

Touraine

Anjou-Saumur

Pinot Noir, Pinot Meunier and Chardonnay

- **Coteaux Champenois** AOC

Champagne

KEY

- Full-bodied
- Medium-bodied
- Light-bodied

Red Wine Appellations of Jura & Savoie

Trousseau	Poulsard	Pinot Noir	Gamay, Mondeuse and Pinot Noir	Gamay

| **Côtes du Jura** AOC Trousseau | **Côtes du Jura** AOC Poulsard | **Côtes du Jura** AOC Pinot Noir | **Vin de Savoie** AOC | **Vin de Savoie** AOC Gamay |
| **Arbois AOC** Trousseau | **Arbois** AOC Poulsard | **Arbois** AOC Pinot Noir | May also contain Persan, Cabernet Franc, Cabernet Sauvignon, Étraire de la Dui, Servanin, Joubertin, plus a maximum in total of Aligoté, Altesse, Jacquère, Chardonnay, Mondeuse Blanche, Chasselas, Savagnin, Marsanne and Verdesse | |

Jura

Trousseau, Poulsard, Pinot Noir

		Vin de Savoie AOC Pinot Noir		**Mondeuse**

| **Côtes du Jura** AOC | | | | |
| **Arbois AOC** | | | | **Vin de Savoie** AOC Mondeuse |

Savoie

KEY

 Medium-bodied

 Light-bodied

Grenache Noir and Mourvèdre blends

Collioure AOC

At least 60% in total of Grenache Noir and Mourvèdre, with at least 25% in total of Carignan, Cinsault and Syrah

Grenache Noir dominated blends

Banyuls AOC

At least 50% Grenache Noir, with Grenache Gris, Grenache Blanc, Macabéo, Tourbat, Muscat Blanc à Petit Grains and Muscat d'Alexandrie, with up to 10% in total of Carignan, Cinsault and Syrah

Banyuls Grand Cru AOC

As Banyuls AOC but with at least 75% Grenache Noir

Maury AOC

At least 75% Grenache Noir, up to 10% Macabéo, and Grenache Gris, Grenache Blanc, Muscat Blanc à Petit Grains, Muscat d'Alexandrie and Tourbat, with up to 10% in total of Carignan, Cinsault, Syrah and Listran Negra

Rivesaltes (Rancio) AOC

May also use Muscat Blanc à Petit Grains, Muscat d'Alexandrie, Grenache Gris, Grenache Blanc, Macabéo, Tourbat, plus up to 10% in total Carignan, Cinsault, Syrah and Palomino

Carignan dominated blends

Côtes du Roussillon AOC

Up to 60% Carignan, with at least 20% Syrah and at least 20% Mourvèdre (no two of these three varieties combined may be more than 90%), up to 10% Macabéo, with Cinsault, Grenache Noir and Lladoner Pelut

Côtes du Roussillon Villages (Caramany) AOC

As Côtes du Rousillon AOC except at least 15% Syrah and at least 15% Mourvèdre

Côtes du Roussillon Vill. Latour-de-France AOC

As Côtes du Rousillon Villages AOC

Fitou AOC

At least 90% in total of Carignan, Grenache Noir and Lladoner Pelut, although the Carignan must be no more than 75%, with up to 10% in total of Cinsault, Macabéo, Mourvèdre, Syrah and Terret Noir

Roussillon

Costières de Nîmes AOC

Up to 40% Carignan, with up to 40% Cinsault, at least 25% Grenache Noir, and at least 20% in total of Mourvèdre and Syrah

Minervois AOC

Up to 40% Carignan, with at least 60% in total of Grenache Noir, Lladoner Pelut, Syrah and Mourvèdre, plus Cinsault, Picpoul Noir, Terret Noir and Aspiran Noir

Corbières AOC

At least 40% Carignan (60% in some areas), plus Macabéo and Bourboulenc which together can be no more than the Carignan, with at least 25% (35% in some areas) in total of Grenache Noir, Lladoner Pelut, and Syrah, plus Mourvèdre, Picpoul, Terret and up to 20% Cinsault

Languedoc

Grenache Noir, Lladoner Pelut, Mourvèdre and Syrah blends

St.-Chinian AOC

At least 50% in total of Grenache Noir, Lladoner Pelut, Mourvèdre and Syrah, with up to 40% Carignan and up to 30% Cinsault

Coteaux du Languedoc (village name) AOC

At least 40% in total of Grenache Noir, Lladoner Pelut, Mourvèdre and Syrah, with up to 40% in total of Carignan and Cinsault, and up to 10% in total of Counoise, Grenache Gris, Terret Noir and Picpoul Noir

Faugères AOC

Up to 30% Carignan, up to 30% Cinsault, at least 20% in total of Grenache Noir and Lladoner Pelut, at least 5% Mourvèdre, and Syrah which together with the Mourvèdre must be at least 15%

KEY

- ■ Full-bodied
- ■ Medium-bodied
- ■ Light-bodied
- ■ Sweet Fortified

Red Wine Appellations of South-West France

Fer Servadou	Tannat	Cabernet Sauvignon, Cabernet Franc and Merlot	Négrette	Malbec

Marcillac AOC

At least 90% Fer, blended with Cabernet Franc, Cabernet Sauvignon and Merlot

Gaillac AOC

At least 20% Fer, with at least 20% Duras and Syrah to make minimum 60%, blended with Cabernet Sauvignon, Cabernet Franc, Merlot and Gamay

Tarn & Aveyron

Béarn (-Bellocq) AOC

At least 60% Tannat, blended with Cabernet Franc, Cabernet Sauvignon, Fer Servadou, Manseng Noir and Courbu Noir

Madiran AOC

At least 40% Tannat, blended with Cabernet Franc, Cabernet Sauvignon, and Fer Servadou

Irouléguy AOC

Blended with a minimum 50% in total of Cabernet Franc and Cabernet Sauvignon

Pyrénées

Buzet AOC

Côtes du Marmandais AOC

Blended with between 25% and 50% in total of Arbouriou, Malbec, Fer, Gamay and Syrah

Côtes de Duras AOC

Bergerac AOC

May also contain Fer and Mérille

Côtes de Bergerac AOC

May also contain Fer and Mérille

Pécharmant AOC

Dordogne

Côtes du Frontonnais AOC

Between 50% and 70% Négrette blended with a maximum 25% in total of Malbec, Mérille, Fer, Syrah, Cabernet Sauvignon and Cabernet Franc, and a maximum 15% in total of Gamay, Cinsault and Mauzac

Garonne

Cahors AOC

At least 70% Malbec, blended with Merlot, Tannat and Jurançon Noir

Lot

KEY

■ Full-bodied

▨ Medium-bodied

▫ Light-bodied

Mourvèdre

Bandol AOC

At least 50% Mourvèdre, with Grenache Noir and Cinsault, up to 10% Syrah and up to 10% Carignan, although these two must be no more than 15% of the total

Grenache Noir

Coteaux d'Aix-en-Provence AOC

At least 60% Grenache Noir, with Cinsault, Counoise, Mourvèdre, Syrah, up to 30% Cabernet Sauvignon and up to 30% Carignan

Provence

Mourvèdre and Grenache Noir

Palette AOC

At least 50% in total of Grenache Noir, Mourvèdre and Cinsault, with Téoulier, Durif, Muscat (any variety), Carignan, Syrah, Castets, Brun Fourca, Terret Gris, Petit-Brun, Tibouren, Cabernet Sauvignon, and up to 15% in total of Clairette, Picardan, Ugni Blanc, Ugni Rosé, Grenache Blanc, Picpoul, Pascal, Aragnan, Colombard and Terret-Bourret

Les Baux de Provence AOC

At least 60% in total of Grenache Noir, Mourvèdre and Syrah, with Cinsault, Counoise, Carignan and Cabernet Sauvignon

Coteaux Varois AOC

At least 80% in total of Grenache Noir, Mourvèdre and Syrah, with Cinsault, Carignan and Cabernet Sauvignon

Cassis AOC

At least 90% in total of Grenache Noir, Mourvèdre, Carignan, Cinsault and Barbarossa, with Terret Noir, Terret Gris, Terret Blanc, Terret Ramenée, Aramon and Aramon Gris

Carignan

Côtes de Provence AOC

Up to 40% Carignan, with Cinsault, Grenache Noir, Mourvèdre, Tibouren and up to 30% Syrah, and up to 30% in total of Barbarossa Rosé, Cabernet Sauvignon, Calitor, Clairette, Sémillon, Ugni Blanc and Vermentino

Braquet, Fuella and Cinsault

Bellet AOC

At least 60% in total of Braquet, Fuella and Cinsault, with Grenache Noir, Vermentino, Ugni Blanc, Mayorquin, Clairette, Bourboulenc, Chard-onnay, Pignerol and Muscat à Petits Grains

Sciacarello and Nielluccio

Ajaccio AOC

At least 40% Sciacarello, which together with Barbarossa, Nielluccio and Vermentino must be more than 60% of the total, with a maximum of 40% in total of Grenache Noir, Cinsault, and up to 15% Carignan

Patrimonio AOC

At least 90% Nielluccio, with Grenache Noir, Sciacarello and Vermentino

Vin de Corse (village name) AOC

At least 50% in total of Nielluccio, Sciacarello and Grenache Noir, with Cinsault, Mourvèdre, Barbarossa, Syrah and up to 20% in total of Carignan and Vermentino

Corsica

KEY

■ Full-bodied

■ Medium-bodied

□ Light-bodied

White Wine Appellations of Burgundy

Pure Chardonnay	Chardonnay & Pinot Blanc	Aligoté & Chardonnay

Pouilly-Fuissé AOC	**Pouilly-Vinzelles** AOC	**Mâcon** (village name) AOC	**Mâcon Villages** AOC	**Bourgogne** (village name) AOC	**Bourgogne-Aligoté** AOC
Pouilly-Loché AOC	**St.-Véran** AOC	**Mâcon Supérieur** AOC	**Viré-Clessé** AOC		Only up to 15% Chardonnay

Mâconnais

Generic Burgundy

Bourgogne Grand-Ordinaire AOC

May also use Pinot Blanc, Melon de Bourgogne, Sacy

Côte Chalonnaise

Chablis

Côtes de Nuits

Chablis (Premier Cru) AOC	**Marsannay (La Côte)** AOC	**Bourgogne Hautes-Côtes de Nuits** AOC	**Morey-St.-Denis** (Premier Cru) AOC	**Givry** (Premier Cru) AOC
Chablis Grand Cru AOC		**Côtes Nuits-Villages** AOC	**Nuits (-St.-George)** (Premier Cru) AOC	**Mercurey** (Premier Cru) AOC
Petit Chablis AOC	**(Le) Musigny Grand Cru** AOC	**Fixin** (Premier Cru) AOC	**Vougeot** (Premier Cru) AOC	**Montagny** (Premier Cru) AOC
Vézelay AOC				**Rully** (Premier Cru) AOC

Bouzeron AOC

Only up to 15% Chardonnay

With Melon de Bourgogne

Côtes de Beaune

Bâtard-Montrachet Grand Cru AOC	**Aloxe-Corton** (Premier Cru) AOC	**Auxey-Duresses** (Premier Cru) AOC	**Côtes de Beaune** AOC	**Beaujolais** AOC
Chevalier-Montrachet Grand Cru AOC	**Charlemagne Grand Cru** AOC	**Beaune** (Premier Cru) AOC	**Ladoix** (Premier Cru) AOC	**Pernand-Vergelesses** (Premier Cru) AOC	**Beaujolais Supérieur** AOC
Bienvenues-Bâtard-Montrachet G. C. AOC	**(Le) Corton Grand Cru** AOC	**Bourgogne Haute-Côtes de Beaune** AOC	**Maranges** (Premier Cru) AOC	**St.-Aubin** (Premier Cru) AOC	**Beaujolais-Villages** AOC
(Le) Montrachet Grand Cru AOC	**Corton-Charlemagne Grand Cru** AOC	**Chorey-Lès-Beaune** AOC	**Meursault** (Premier Cru) AOC	**St.-Romain** AOC	**Coteaux du Lyonnais** AOC
	Criots-Bâtard-Montrachet G. C. AOC	**Chassagne-Montrachet** (Premier Cru) AOC	**Meursault-Blagny** Premier Cru AOC	**Santenay** (Premier Cru) AOC	
		Puligny-Montrachet (Premier Cru) AOC	**Monthelie** (Premier Cru) AOC	**Savigny-Lès-Beaune** (Premier Cru) AOC	

Beaujolais

KEY

☐ Dry

White Wine Appellation Hierarchy of Burgundy (1/2)

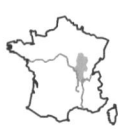

Côtes de Beaune

Grands Crus	Bâtard-Montrachet Chevalier-Montrachet Bienvenues-Bâtard-Montrachet (Le) Montrachet	Criots-Bâtard-Montrachet	Charlemagne Corton Corton-Charlemagne			
Premiers Crus	Puligny-Montrachet Premier Cru	Chassagne-Montrachet Premier Cru	Aloxe-Corton Premier Cru	Auxey-Duresses Premier Cru Beaune Premier Cru Ladoix Premier Cru Maranges Premier Cru Monthelie Premier Cru Pernand-Vergelesses Premier Cru St.-Aubin Premier Cru Santenay Premier Cru Savigny (-Lès-Beaune) Premier Cru	Meursault Premier Cru Meursault Blagny Premier Cru	
Village Wines	Puligny-Montrachet	Chassagne-Montrachet	Aloxe-Corton	Auxey-Duresses Beaune Ladoix Maranges Monthelie Pernand-Vergelesses St.-Aubin Santenay Savigny (-Lès-Beaune)	Meursault	Bourgogne Haute-Côtes de Beaune Côtes de Beaune Chorey-Lès-Beaune St.-Romain
	Bourgogne Grand-Ordinaire / Bourgogne <Village Name>					
Basic	Bourgogne / Bourgogne Aligoté					

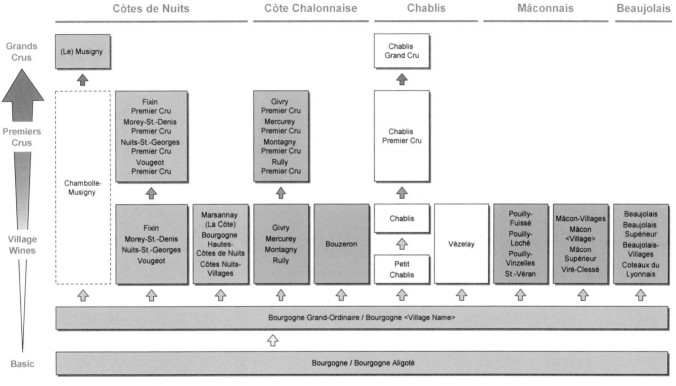

	Côtes de Nuits	Côte Chalonnaise	Chablis	Mâconnais	Beaujolais

Grands Crus

(Le) Musigny

Chablis Grand Cru

Premiers Crus

Chambolle-Musigny

Fixin Premier Cru
Morey-St.-Denis Premier Cru
Nuits-St.-Georges Premier Cru
Vougeot Premier Cru

Givry Premier Cru
Mercurey Premier Cru
Montagny Premier Cru
Rully Premier Cru

Chablis Premier Cru

Village Wines

Fixin
Morey-St.-Denis
Nuits-St.-Georges
Vougeot

Marsannay (La Côte)
Bourgogne Hautes-Côtes de Nuits
Côtes Nuits-Villages

Givry
Mercurey
Montagny
Rully

Bouzeron

Chablis

Petit Chablis

Vézelay

Pouilly-Fuissé
Pouilly-Loché
Pouilly-Vinzelles
St.-Véran

Mâcon-Villages
Mâcon <Village>
Mâcon Supérieur
Viré-Clessé

Beaujolais
Beaujolais Supérieur
Beaujolais-Villages
Coteaux du Lyonnais

Bourgogne Grand-Ordinaire / Bourgogne <Village Name>

Basic

Bourgogne / Bourgogne Aligoté

Côte de Beaune

Aloxe-Corton

Les Chaillots, La Coutière, Les Fournières, Les Guérets, La Maréchaude, Clos des Maréchaudes, Les Maréchaudes, Les Meix/Clos du Chapitre, Les Moutottes, Les Paulards, Les Petites Lolières, La Toppe au Vert, Les Valozières, Les Vercots

Auxey-Duresses

Bas des Duresses, Les Bretterins, La Chapelle, Climat du Val, Les Duresses, Les Écusseaux, Les Grands-Champs, Reugne

Beaune

Les Aigrots, Aux Coucherias/Clos de la Féguine, Aux Cras, Clos des Avaux, Les Avaux, Le Bas de Teurons, Les Beaux Fougets, Belissand, Les Blanches Fleurs, Les Champs Pimont, Les Chouacheux, l'Écu/Clos de l'Écu, Les Epenottes/ Les Epenotes, Les Fèves, En Genêt, Les Grèves, Clos Landry/Clos Ste.-Landry, Les Longes, Le Clos des Mouches, Les Clos de la Mousse, Les Marconnets, Le Mignotte, Montée Rouge, Les Montrevenots, En l'Orme, Les Perrières, Pertuisots, Les Reversées, Clos du Roi, Les Seurey, Les Sizies, Clos Ste.-Anne/Sur les Grèves, Les Teurons, Les Toussaints, Les Tuvilains, Le Vigne de l'Enfant Jésus, Les Vignes Franches/Clos des Ursules

Chassagne-Montrachet

Abbaye de Morgeot, Les Baudines, Blanchot Dessus, Les Boirettes, Bois de Chassagne, Les Bondues, La Boudriotte, Les Brussonnes, En Cailleret, La Cardeuse, Champ Jendreau, Les Champs Gain, La Chapelle, Clos Chareau, Les Chaumées, Les Chaumes, Les Chenevottes, Les Combards, Les Commes, Ez Crets, Ez Crottes, Dent de Chien, Les Embrazées, Les Fairendes, Francemont, Le Grande Borne, La Grande Montagne, Les Grandes Ruchottes, Les Grand Clos, Guerchère, Les Macherelles, La Maltroie, Les Morgeots, Les Murées, Les Pasquelles, Petingeret, Les Petites Fairendes, Les Petits Clos, Clos Pitois, Les Places, Les Rebichets, En Remilly, La Romanée, La Roquemaure, Clos St.-Jean, Tête du Clos, Tonton Marcel, Les Vergers, Vide Bourse, Vigne Blanche, Vigne Derrière, En Virondot

Ladoix

Basses Mourottes, Bois Roussot, Les Buis, Le Clou d'Orge, La Corvée, Les Gréchons, Hautes Mourottes, Les Joyeuses, La Micaude, En Naget, Rognet et Corton

Maranges

Clos de la Boutière, La Croix Moines, La Fussière, Le Clos des Loyères, Le Clos des Rois, Les Clos Roussots

Meursault

Aux Perrières, Les Bouchères, Les Caillerets, Les Charmes-Dessous/Les Charmes-Dessus, Les Chaumes de Narvaux, Les Chaumes de Perrières, Les Cras, Les Genevrières-Dessous/ Les Genevrières-Dessus, Les Gouttes d'Or, La Jeunelotte, Clos des Perrières, Les Perrières-Dessous/Les Perrières-Dessus, La Pièce sous le Bois, Les Plures, Le Porusot, Les Porusot-Dessous/Les Porusot-Dessus, Clos des Richemont/Cras, Les Santenots Blancs, Les Santenots du Milieu', Sous Blagny, Sous le Dos d'Âne

Meursault-Blagny

La Jeunelotte, La Pièce sous le Bois, Sous Blagny, Sous le Dos d'Ane

Monthelie

La Cas Rougeot, Les Champs Fuillot, Les Duresses, La Château Gaillard, Le Clos Gauthey, Le Meix Bataille, Les Riottes, Sur la Velle, La Taupine, Les Vignes Rondes, Le Village do Monthelie

Pernand Vergelesses

En Caradeux, Creux de la Net, Les Fichots, Île des Hautes Vergelesses, Les Basses Vergelesses

Puligny-Montrachet

Le Cailleret/Demoiselles, Les Chalumeaux, Champ Canet, Champ Gain, Au Chaniot, Clavaillon, Les Combettes, Ez Folatières, Les Folatières, (Sur) la Garenne, Clos de la Garenne, Hameau de Blagny, La Jaquelotte, Clos des Meix, Clos de la Mouchère/Les Perrières, Peux Bois, Les Pucelles, Les Referts, En la Richarde, Sous le Courthil, Sous le Puits, La Truffière

St.-Aubin

La Bas de Gamay à l'Est, Bas de Vermarain à l'Est, Les Castets, Les Cahmplots, En Champs, Le Charmois, La Chatenière, Les Combes au Sud, Les Cortons, En Créot, Derrière chez Edouard, Derrière la Tour, Echaille, Les Frionnes, Sur Gamay, Marinot, En Montceau, Les Murgers des Dents de Chien, Les Perrières, Pitangeret, Le Puits, En la Ranché, En Remilly, Sous Roche Dumay, Sur le Sentier du Clou, Les Travers de Marinot, Vignes Moingeon, Le Village, En Vollon à l'Est

Santenay

Beauregard, Le Chainey, La Comme, Comme Dessus, Clos Faubard, Les Fourneaux, Grand Clos Rousseau, Les Gravières, La Maladière, Clos de Mouches, Passetemps, Petit Clos Rousseau, Clos de Tavannes

Savigny-Lès-Beaune

Aux Clous, Aux Fournaux, Aux Gravains, Aux Guettes, Aux Serpentières, Bas Marconnets, Basses Vergelesses, Clos la Bataillères/Les Vergelesses, Champ Chevrey/Aux Fournaux, Les Charnières, Hauts Jarrons/La Dominodes, Les Lavières, Les Narbantons, Petits Godeaux, Les Peuillets, Redrescut, Les Rouvrettes, Les Talmettes

Chablis

Chablis

Grands Crus
Blanchot, Bougros, Les Clos, Grenouilles, Les Preuses, Valmur, Vaudésir

Premiers Crus
Les Beauregards, Beauroy, Berdiot, Chaume de Talvat, Côte de Jouan, Côte de Léchet, Côte de Vaubarousse, Fouchaume, Les Fourneaux, Montée de Tonnerre, Montmains, Mont de Milieu, Vaillons, Vaucoupin, Vau-de-Vey/Vaudevey, Vau Ligneau, Vosgros

White Wine Premiers Crus and Villages of Burgundy (2/2)

| Côte de Nuits | Côte Chalonnaise | Generic Burgundy |

Fixin

Les Arvelets, Clos du Chapitre, Clos de la Perrière (m), Aux Cheusots, Les Hervelets, Le Meix Bas, La Perrière, Queue de Hareng, En Suchot, Le Village

Vougeot

Les Crâs, Clos de la Perrière, Les Petit Vougeots, La Vigne Blanche

Morey-St.-Denis

Clos Baulet, Les Blanchards, La Bussière, Les Chaffots, Aux Charmes, Les Charrières, Les Chénevery, Aux Cheseaux, Les Faconnières, Les Genevrières, Les Gruenchers, Les Millandes, Monts Luisants, Clos des Ormes, Clos Sorbè, Les Sorbès, Côte Rôtie, La Riotte, Les Ruchots, Le Village

Nuits-St.-Georges

Les Argillats, Les Argillières, Clos Arlot, Aux Boudots, Aux Bousselots, Les Cailles, Les Chaboeufs, Aux Chaignots, Chaine-Carteau/Chaines-Carteaux, Aux Champs Perdrix, Clos des Corvées, Clos des Corvées Pagets, Aux Cras, Les Crots, Les Damodes, Les Didiers, Les Forêts/Clos des Forêts St.-Georges, Les Grandes Vignes, Château Gris, Les Hauts Pruliers, Clos de la Maréchale, Aux Murgers, Aux Perdrix, En la Perrière Noblet, Les Perrières, Les Porets, Les Poulettes, Les Procès, Les Pruliers, La Richemone, La Roncière, Rue de Chaux, Les St.-Georges, Clos St.-Marc/Aux Corvées, Les Terres Blanches, Aux Thorey, Les Vallerots, Les Vaucrains, Aux Vignerondes

Givry

Clos de la Barraude, Les Berges, Bois Chevaux, Bois Gauthier, Clos de Cellier aux Moines, Clos Charlé, Clos du Cras Long, Les Grandes Vignes, Grands Prétants, Clos Jus, Clos Marceaux, Marole, Petit Marole, Petit Prétants, Clos St.-Paul, Clos St.-Pierre, Clos Salomon, Clos de la Servoisine, Vaux, Clos de Vernoy, En Vignes Rouge, Le Vigron

Mercurey

La Bondue, Les Byots, La Cailloute, Champs Martins, La Chassière, Le Clos, Clos des Barraults, Clos Château de Montaigu, Clos l'Evêque, Clos de Myglands, Clos du Roi, Clos Tonnere, Clos Voyens/Les Voyens, Les Combins, Les Crêts, Les Criochots, Les Fourneaux/Clos des Fourneaux, Grand Clos Fortoul, Les Grands Voyens, Griffères, Le Levrière, Le Marcilly/Clos Marcilly, La Mission, Les Montaigus/Clos des Montaigus, Les Naugues, Les Petits Voyens, Les Ruelles, Sazenay, Les Vasées, Les Velley

Montagny

Les Bassets, Les Beaux Champs, Les Bonnevaux, Les Bordes, Les Bouchots, Le Breuil, Les Burnins, Les Carlins, Les Champs-Toiseau, Les Charmelottes, Les Chandits, Les Chazelles, Clos Chaudron, Le Choux, Les Clouzeaux, Les Coères, Les Combes, La Condemine, Cornevent, La Corvée, Les Coudrettes, Les Craboulettes, Les Crets, Creux des Beaux Champs, L'Épaule, Les Garchères, Les Gouresses, La Grand Pièce, Les Jardins, Les Males, Les Marais, Les Marocs, Les Monts Cuchots, Le Mont Laurent, La Mouillère, Moulin l'Echenaud, Les Pandars, Les Pasquires, Les Pidans, Les Platières, Les Resses, Les St.-Mortille, Les St.-Ytages, Sous les Roches, Les Thilles, La Tillone, Les Treufferes, Les Varignys, Le Vieux Château, Vignes Blanche, Vignes sue le Clou, Les Vignes Couland, Les Vignes Derrière, Vignes Longues, Vignes du Puits, Les Vignes St.-Pierre, Les Vignes du Soleil

Rully

Agneux, Bas de Vauvry, la Bressaude, Champ-Clou, Chapitre, Clos du Chaigne, Clos St.-Jacques, Cloux/Les Cloux, Ecloseaux, La Fosse, Grésigny, Margotey/Margoté, Marissou, Meix-Caillet, Mont-Palais, Moulesne/Molesme, Phillot, Les Pieres, Pillot, Préau, La Pucelle, Raboursay/Rabourcé, Raclot, La Renarde, Vauvry

Bourgogne Villages

Côte de Beaune
La Chapelle Notre-Dame

Côtes de Nuits
La Chapitre, Montrecul/Montre-cul/En Montre-cul

Chablis
Côtes d'Auxerre, Chitry, Coulanges-la-Vineuse, Epineuil, Irancy, Saint-Bris, Côte St.-Jacques

Mâconnais

Mâcon Villages

Azé, Berzé-le-Ville, Bissy-La-Mâconnaise, Burgy, Busières, Chaintre, Chânes, Chapelle-de-Guinchay, Chardonnay, Charnay-Lès-Mâcon, Chasselas, Chevagny-Lès-Chevrières, Crèches-sur-Saône, Cruzille, Davayé, Fuissé, Grévilly, Hurigny, Igé, Leynes, Loché, Lugny, Milly-Lamartine, Montbellet, Péronne, Pierreclos, Prissé, Pruzilly, La Roche Vineuse, Romanèche-Thorins, St.-Amour-Bellevue, St.-Gengoux-de-Scissé, St.-Symphorien-d'Ancelles, St.-Vérand, Sologny, Solutré, Uchizy, Vergisson, Verzé, Vinzelles

Beaujolais

Beaujolais Villages

Arbuisonnas, Les Ardillats, Beaujeu, Blacé, Chânes, Charentay, Chénas, Denicé, Durette, Lancié, Lantignié, Marchampt, Montmelas, Odenas, Le Perréon, Rivolet, St.Étiennes-des-Ouillères, St-Julien, St.-Lager, Salles, Vaux, Vauxrenard

Note: it is possible to find other village names under the Beaujolais (village name) AOC, but these others are allowed to use higher priced appellations including Cru Beaujolais, Mâcon-Villages AOC and St.-Veran AOC, so seldom use village Beaujolais

33

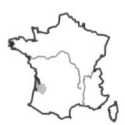

White Wine Appellations of Bordeaux

Sémillon and Sauvignon Blanc, blended with Muscadelle

Graves

- **Graves** AOC
- **Graves Supérieur** AOC
- **Pessac-Léognan** AOC

Minimum 25% Sauvignon Blanc

- **Cérons** AOC
- **Barsac** AOC
- **Sauternes** AOC

Entre-Deux-Mers

- **Bordeaux Haut-Benauge** AOC
- **Premières-Côtes-de-Bordeaux** AOC
- **Cadillac** AOC
- **Côtes de Bordeaux-St.-Macaire** AOC
- **Loupiac** AOC
- **St.-Croix-du-Mont** AOC

Libournais

- **Bordeaux-Côtes-de-Francs** AOC
- **Bordeaux-Côtes-de-Francs Liquoreux** AOC

Blaye

- **Premières Côtes de Blaye** AOC

Sémillon and Sauvignon Blanc, blended with Muscadelle, Merlot Blanc and Colombard

Entre-Deux-Mers

- **Entre-Deux-Mers** AOC

With up to 30% Merlot Blanc and up to 10% other varieties including Mauzac

- **Entre-Deux-Mers-Haut-Benauge** AOC

As Entre-Deux-Mers AOC

- **Ste.-Foy-Bordeaux** AOC

With up to 10% other varieties including Mauzac

- **Graves de Vayres** AOC

With up to 30% Merlot Blanc

Generic Bordeaux

- **Bordeaux** AOC

With up to 30% other varieties including Mauzac, Ondenc and Ugni Blanc

- **Bordeaux Supérieur** AOC

As Bordeaux AOC but only up to 15% Merlot Blanc

Bourg

- **Côtes de Bourg** AOC

With up to 10% Chenin Blanc

Blaye

- **Blaye/Blayais** AOC

Predominantly Sauvignon Blanc, may also include Chenin Blanc, Ugni Blanc and Folle Blanche

- **Côtes de Blaye** AOC

As Blaye AOC without Ugni Blanc

KEY

- Sweet
- Semi-Sweet
- Off-Dry
- Dry

White Wine Producer Classifications of Bordeaux

Graves

Sauternes	Barsac	Graves
Premier Cru Supérieur Château d'Yquem **Premier Cru** Château La Tour Blanche, Château Lafaurie-Payraguey, Château Clos Haut-Payraguey, Château Rayne-Vigneau, Château Suduiraut, Château Guiraud, Château Rieussec, Château Rabaud-Promis, Château Sigelas-Rabaud **Deuxième Cru** Château d'Arche, Château Filhot, Château de Malle, Château Romer, Château Romer-du-Hayot, Château Lamothe, Château Lamothe-Guignard	**Premier Cru** Château Coutet, Château Climens **Deuxième Cru** Château Myrat, Château Doisy-Daëne, Château Doisy-Dubroca, Château Doisy-Védrines, Château Broustet, Château Nairac, Château Caillou, Château Suau	**Cru Classé** Château Bouscaut, Château Carbonnieux, Domaine de Chevalier, Château Couhins-Lurton, Château Haut-Brion, Château Laville Haut-Brion, Château Malartic-Lagravière, Château Olivier, Château La Tour-Martillac

White Wine Appellations of the Rhône

Bourboulenc and Clairette

Côtes du Ventoux AOC

At least 70% Bourboulenc and Clairette blended with Grenache Blanc and Roussanne

Côtes-du-Rhône-Villages AOC

At least 80% Clairette, Roussanne and Bourboulenc, with up to 10% Grenache Blanc and up to 10% other varieties including Ugni Blanc, Viognier, Carignan, Pinot Blanc, Mauzac, Pascal Blanc, Calitor, Gamay, Camarèse

Muscat Blanc à Petit Grains

Muscat de Beaumes-de-Venise AOC

Southern Rhône

Grenache Blanc, Roussanne and Bourboulenc

Châteauneuf-du-Pape AOC

May also use Syrah, Mourvèdre, Picpoul, Terret Noir, Counoise, Muscardin, Vaccarèse, Picardan, Cinsault and Clairette

Côtes-du-Rhône AOC

At least 40% Grenache Blanc, Clairette, Syrah, Mourvèdre, Picpoul, Terret Noir, Picardan, Cinsault, Roussanne, Marsanne, Bourboulenc, Viognier, with up to 30% Carignan and up to 30% Counoise, Muscardin, Vaccarèse, Pinot Blanc, Mauzac, Pascal Blanc, Ugni Blanc, Calitor, Gamay and Camarèse

Grenache Gris or Grenache Blanc

Rasteau (Rancio) AOC

At least 90% Grenache (Gris or Blanc), with up to 10% other varieties including Picardan, Ugni Blanc, Viognier, Carignan, Pinot Blanc, Calitor, Gamay, Camarèse, Mauzac, Pascal Blanc

Grenache Blanc and Clairette

Coteaux du Tricastin AOC

May also use Picpoul Blanc, Bourboulenc, Ugni Blanc, Roussanne, Viognier, Marsanne

Côtes du Lubéron AOC

May also use Roussanne, Ugni Blanc, Vermentino, Bourboulenc, Marsanne

Lirac AOC

May also use Bourboulenc, but no single variety more than 60%, with up to 30% Ugni Blanc, Picpoul, Marsanne, Roussanne, Viognier

Vacqueyras AOC

May also use Bourboulenc, Marsanne, Roussanne, Viognier

Marsanne and/or Roussanne

Rousanne dominated wines tend to be finer, and Marsanne dominated wines tend to be richer

St.-Joseph AOC

St.-Péray AOC

Crozes-Hermitage AOC

Hermitage AOC

Hermitage Vin de Paille AOC

Viognier

Condrieu AOC

Château Grillet AOC

Clairette

Coteaux de Die AOC

Aligoté

Châtillon-en-Diois AOC Aligoté

Chardonnay

Châtillon-en-Diois AOC Chardonnay

Northern Rhône

KEY

 Sweet Fortified

 Dry

White Wine Appellations of the Loire & Champagne

Melon de Bourgogne

Muscadet AOC
Muscadet Coteaux de la Loire AOC

May also be "sur lie" after a winter on its lees

Muscadet Côtes de Grandlieu AOC

May also be "sur lie" after a winter on its lees

Muscadet de Sèvre-et-Maine AOC

May also be "sur lie" after a winter on its lees

Pays Nantais

Chardonnay, Pinot Noir and Pinot Meunier

Coteaux Champenois AOC

Champagne

Chenin Blanc

Savennières AOC
Saumur AOC

With up to 20% Chardonnay and/or Sauvignon Blanc

Anjou Coteaux de la Loire AOC
Anjou AOC

With up to 20% Chardonnay and/or Sauvignon Blanc

Coteaux de l'Aubance AOC
Coteaux de Saumur AOC
Bonnezeaux AOC
Coteaux du Layon AOC
Coteaux du Layon-Chaume AOC
Coteaux du Layon Villages AOC

Anjou-Saumur

Coteaux de Loir AOC
Touraine-Amboise AOC
Chinon AOC
Touraine-Mesland AOC
Touraine Azay-le-Rideau AOC
Jasnières AOC
Montlouis AOC
Vouvray AOC

May contain Arbois

Touraine

Quarts-de-Chaume AOC

Sauvignon Blanc

Touraine AOC

May use some Chenin Blanc or Arbois and up to 20% Chardonnay

Cheverny AOC

May use up to 35% Chardonnay, Chenin Blanc and/or Arbois

Menetou-Salon AOC
Quincy AOC
Reuilly AOC
Sancerre AOC
Pouilly-Fumé AOC
Coteaux du Giennois AOC

Central Vineyards

Romordantin

Cour-Cheverny AOC

Chasselas

Pouilly-sur-Loire AOC

With some Sauvignon Blanc

KEY

☐ Sweet
☐ Semi-Sweet
▨ Dry
☐ Bone Dry

Gewürztraminer

(Vin d') **Alsace** AOC
Gewürztraminer

Alsace Grand Cru AOC
Gewürztraminer

Alsace Gewürztraminer
Vendage Tardives

Alsace Gr. Cru Gewürz.
Vendage Tardives

Alsace Gewürztraminer
Sélection de Grains Nobles

Alsace Gr. Cru Gewürz.
Sélection de Grains Nobles

Muscat varieties

These wines may be made from
Muscat d'Alsace (same as Muscat à
Petit Grains, either Blanc or Rosé
varieties), or Muscat Ottonel

(Vin d') **Alsace** AOC
Muscat

Alsace Grand Cru AOC
Muscat

Alsace AOC Muscat
Vendage Tardives

Alsace Grand Cru AOC
Muscat Vendage Tardives

Alsace AOC Muscat
Sélection de Grains Nobles

Alsace Grand Cru Muscat
Sélection de Grains Nobles

Pinot Gris

This grape variety may also be called
Tokay, or Tokay-Pinot-Gris

(Vin d') **Alsace** AOC
Pinot Gris

Alsace Grand Cru AOC
Pinot Gris

Alsace AOC Pinot Gris
Vendage Tardives

Alsace Grand Cru Pinot
Gris Vendage Tardives

Alsace AOC Pinot Gris
Sélection de Grains Nobles

Alsace Gr. Cru Pinot Gris
Sélection de Grains Nobles

Riesling

(Vin d') **Alsace** AOC
Riesling

Alsace Grand Cru AOC
Riesling

Alsace AOC Riesling
Vendage Tardives

Alsace Grand Cru AOC
Riesling Vendage Tardives

Alsace AOC Riesling
Sélection de Grains Nobles

Alsace Grand Cru Riesling
Sélection de Grains Nobles

Blends

May contain Chasselas, Sylvaner,
Pinot Blanc, Pinot Noir, Auxerrois,
Gewürztraminer, Muscat Blanc à Petit
Grains, Muscat Rosé à Petit Grains,
Muscat Ottonel, Riesling

(Vin d') **Alsace** AOC

Edelzwicker AOC

KEY

☐ Sweet

▨ Off-Dry

☐ Dry

Auxerrois

(Vin d') **Alsace** AOC
Auxerrois

Chasselas

(Vin d') **Alsace** AOC
Chasselas

Sylvaner

(Vin d') **Alsace** AOC
Sylvaner

Pinot Blanc

(Vin d') **Alsace** AOC
Pinot Blanc

(Vin d') **Alsace** AOC
Pinot/Clevner/Klevner

May also contain Auxerrois, Pinot
Noir, Pinot Gris

Savagnin Rosé

**Klevener de
Heiligenstein** AOC

White Wine Appellations of Jura & Savoie

Chasselas

Crépy AOC

Vin de Savoie AOC Marignan

Vin de Savoie AOC Ripaille

Savoie

Roussanne

Vin de Savoie AOC Bergeron

Vin de Savoie AOC Chignin-Bergeron

Altesse

Seyssel AOC

Vin de Savoie AOC

May also contain Aligoté, Jacquère, Chardonnay, Mondeuse Blanche, Chasselas, Savagnin, Roussette d'Ayze, Marsanne, Verdesse

Roussette de Savoie AOC

Roussette is a local synonym for Altesse, although this wine may also contain Chardonnay and Mondeuse Blanche

Savagnin and/or Chardonnay

Arbois AOC

May also contain Pinot Blanc

Arbois-Pupillin AOC

May also contain Pinot Blanc

Vin Jeune d'Arbois/ Arbois Vin Jeune AOC

Château-Chalon AOC

Côtes du Jura AOC

Côtes du Jura Vin Jeune AOC

L'Etoile AOC

May also contain Poulsard

Vin de Paille de l' Etoile/ L'Etoile Vin de Paille AOC

May also contain Poulsard

Savagnin, Chardonnay, Poulsard & Trousseau

Vin de Paille d'Arbois/ Arbois Vin de Paille AOC

Côtes du Jura Vin de Paille AOC

Pure Savagnin

Vin Jeune de l' Etoile/ L'Etoile Vin Jeune AOC

Jura

KEY

- ▢ Sweet Fortified
- ▢ Sweet
- ▢ Off-Dry
- ▢ Dry

White Wine Appellations of Languedoc-Roussillon

Clairette

Clairette de Bellegarde AOC

Clairette du Languedoc AOC

Languedoc

Muscat varieties

Muscat de Frontignan/ Vin de Frontignan AOC

Uses Muscat Blanc à Petit Grains

Muscat de Lunel AOC

Uses Muscat Blanc à Petit Grains

Muscat de Mireval AOC

Uses Muscat Blanc à Petit Grains

Muscat de St.-Jean- de-Minervois AOC

Uses Muscat Blanc à Petit Grains

Muscat de Risevaltes AOC

Uses Muscat Blanc à Petit Grains and Muscat d'Alexandrie

Rivesaltes AOC

May use Muscat Blanc à Petit Grains, Muscat d'Alexandrie, Macabéo, Tourbat, Grenache Noir, Grenache Gris, Grenache Blanc, Palomino, Ugni Blanc, Chenin Blanc, Cinsault

Roussillon

Grenache Blanc blended with other varieties

Corbières AOC

At least 50% blended with Bourboulenc and Macabéo, may also use Muscat Blanc à Petit Grains Clairette, Picpoul, Terret, Roussanne and Vermentino

Minervois AOC

May also use Macabéo, Clairette, Bourboulenc, Picpoul, Terret, Marsanne, Roussanne, Vermentino and up to 10% Muscat à Petit Grains

Banyuls (Rancio) AOC

May also use Macabéo, Tourbat, Muscat Blanc à Petit Grains and Muscat d'Alexandrie

Banyuls Grand Cru (Rancio) AOC

As Banyuls AOC

Clairette and Ugni Blanc

Costières de Nîmes AOC

May also use Grenache Blanc, Bourboulenc, Marsanne, Roussanne, Macabéo, Vermentino

Coteaux du Languedoc AOC

May also use Grenache Blanc, Bourboulenc, Picpoul, Marsanne, Roussanne, Macabéo, Vermentino, Terret Blanc, Carignan Blanc

Macabéo and Tourbat

Côtes du Roussillon AOC

Chardonnay

Limoux AOC

With at least 15% Mauzac, may also use Chenin Blanc

Grenache Noir

Maury AOC

At least 75% Grenache Noir, up to 10% Macabéo, and Grenache Gris, Grenache Blanc, Muscat Blanc à Petit Grains, Muscat d'Alexandrie and Tourbat, with up to 10% in total of Carignan, Cinsault, Syrah and Listran Negra

KEY

☐ Sweet Fortified

☐ Sweet

☐ Off-Dry

☐ Dry

White Wine Appellations of South-West France

Manseng & Courbu

Béarn (-Bellocq) AOC

May also use Lauzet, Camaralet, Raffiat, Sauvignon Blanc

Irouléguy AOC

Jurançon (Sec) AOC

May also use up to 15% Lauzet, Camaralet

Pacherenc du Vic-Bilh AOC

May also use Sauvignon Blanc, Sémillon, Arrufiac

Pyrénées

Sémillon, Sauvignon Blanc, and Muscadelle

Haut-Montravel AOC

Côtes de Montravel AOC

Monbazillac AOC

Rosette AOC

Buzet AOC

Sauvignon Blanc, Sémillon and Muscadelle blended with other varieties

Bergerac (Sec) AOC

May also use Chenin Blanc, Ugni Blanc, Ondenc

Saussignac AOC

May also use Chenin Blanc

Côtes de Duras AOC

May also use Chenin Blanc, Ugni Blanc, Ondenc, Mauzac

Gaillac Premier Côtes AOC

May also use Ondenc, Mauzac, Len de l'El

Gaillac (Doux) AOC

May also use Ondenc, Mauzac, Len de l'El

Tarn & Aveyron

Sauvignon Blanc blended with other varieties

Montravel AOC

Sauvignon Blanc dominated but may also use Sémillon, Muscadelle, Ondenc and up to 25% Ugni Blanc

Dordogne

Côtes du Marmandais AOC

At least 70% Sauvignon Blanc, and may also use Sémillon, Ugni Blanc

Garonne

KEY

☐ Sweet

☐ Semi-Sweet (Moelleux)

☐ Off-Dry

☐ Dry

41

White Wine Appellations of Provence & Corsica

42

Blends which may include Clairette and Ugni Blanc

Ugni Blanc & Vermentino

Muscat Blanc à Petit Grains

Coteaux d'Aix-en-Provence AOC

May also use Bourboulenc, Sauvignon Blanc, Grenache Blanc, Vermentino, Pascal Blanc

Palette AOC

May also use Picardan, Ugni Rosé, Grenache Blanc, Muscat (any variety), Picpoul, Pascal, Aragnan, Colombard, Terret-Bourret

Provence

(Vin de) Bandol AOC

May also use Bourboulenc, Sauvignon Blanc

(Vin de) Bellet AOC

May also use Bourboulenc, Mayorquin, Chardonnay, Pignerol, Muscat à Petit Grains, Vermentino and Sémillon

Cassis AOC

May also use Sauvignon Blanc, Doucillon, Marsanne, Pascal Blanc

Côtes de Provence AOC

May also use Vermentino, Pascal Blanc

Coteaux Varios AOC

As Cotes de Provence AOC, but may also use Grenache Blanc

Ajaccio AOC

Patrimonio AOC

Vin de Corse (sub-appellation) AOC

Muscat du Cap Corse AOC

Corsica

KEY

Sweet Fortified

Sweet

Off-Dry

Dry

Rosé Wine Appellations of Burgundy & Bordeaux

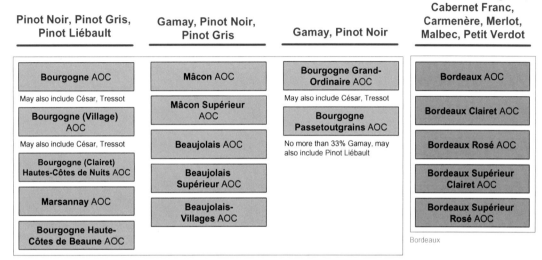

Pinot Noir, Pinot Gris, Pinot Liébault	Gamay, Pinot Noir, Pinot Gris	Gamay, Pinot Noir	Cabernet Sauvignon, Cabernet Franc, Carmenère, Merlot, Malbec, Petit Verdot
Bourgogne AOC	**Mâcon** AOC	**Bourgogne Grand-Ordinaire** AOC	**Bordeaux** AOC
May also include César, Tressot	**Mâcon Supérieur** AOC	May also include César, Tressot	**Bordeaux Clairet** AOC
Bourgogne (Village) AOC	**Beaujolais** AOC	**Bourgogne Passetoutgrains** AOC	**Bordeaux Rosé** AOC
May also include César, Tressot	**Beaujolais Supérieur** AOC	No more than 33% Gamay, may also include Pinot Liébault	**Bordeaux Supérieur Clairet** AOC
Bourgogne (Clairet) Hautes-Côtes de Nuits AOC	**Beaujolais-Villages** AOC		**Bordeaux Supérieur Rosé** AOC
Marsannay AOC			
Bourgogne Haute-Côtes de Beaune AOC			

Bordeaux

Burgundy

KEY

Medium-Dry

Dry

43

Rosé Wine Appellations of the Rhône

Muscat Rosé à Petit Grains

Muscat de Beaumes-de-Venise AOC

Southern Rhône

Grenache Gris or Grenache Blanc

Rasteau (Rancio) AOC

At least 90% Grenache (Gris or Blanc), with up to 10% other varieties including Picpoul, Terret Noir, Picardan, Roussanne, Viognier and the standard Côtes-du-Rhône blending varieties *

Grenache Noir, Syrah and Mourvèdre

Côtes-du-Rhône AOC

May contain Grenache Noir, Clairette, Syrah, Mourvèdre, Picpoul, Terret Noir, Picardan, Roussanne, Marsanne, Borboulenc, Viognier; up to 30% Carignan; up to 30% in total of the standard Côtes-du-Rhône blending varieties *

Côtes du Ventoux AOC

May contain Grenache Noir, Syrah, Cinsault, Mourvèdre, up to 30% Carignan, up to 20% in total of Picpoul Noir, Counoise, Clairette, Bourboulenc, Grenache Blanc and Roussanne

Coteaux du Tricastin AOC

May contain Grenache Noir, Cinsault, Mourvèdre, Syrah, Picpoul Noir; up to 20% Carignan, and up to 20% in total of Grenache Blanc, Clairette, Bourboulenc and Ugni Blanc

Tavel AOC

May contain no more than 60% each of Grenache Noir, Cinsault, Clairette, Clairette Rosé, Picpoul, Calitor, Bourboulenc, Mourvèdre and Syrah, with up to 10% Carignan

Grenache Noir dominated blends

Côtes-du-Rhône-Villages AOC

At least 60% Grenache Noir; up to 10% Carignan; at least 10% Camarèse and Cinsault; up to 10% in total of Picpoul, Terret Noir, Picardan, Roussanne, Marsanne, Vaccarèse, Pinot Blanc, Mauzac, Pascal Blanc, Ugni Blanc, Calitor, Gamay, Mourvèdre, Clairette and Bourboulenc

Gigondas AOC

At least 80% Grenache Noir; may also contain Clairette, Picpoul, Terret Noir, Picardin, Cinsault, Roussanne, Marsanne, Bourboulenc, Viognier and the standard Côtes-du-Rhône blending varieties *

Lirac AOC

At least 40% Grenache Noir; at least 25% Syrah and Mourvèdre; up to 10% Carignan; up to 20% Cinsault; up to 20% in total of Grenache Blanc, Ugni Blanc, Picpoul, Marsanne, Roussanne, Viognier, Clairette and Bourboulenc

Côtes du Lubéron AOC

At least 10% Syrah and at least 60% Grenache Noir and Syrah; up to 40% Mourvèdre; up to 20% Cinsault; up to 20% Carignan; up to 20% in total of Grenache Blanc, Vermentino, Ugni Blanc, Roussanne, Marsanne, Clairette and Bourboulenc

Vacqueyras AOC

At least 60% Grenache Noir; may also contain up to 15% Mourvèdre or Cinsault; up to 15% Terret Noir, Counoise, Muscardin, Vaccarèse, Gamay, Camarèse

* Note: the standard red Côtes-du-Rhône blending varieties are: Counoise, Muscardin, Vaccarèse, Pinot Blanc, Mauzac, Pascal Blanc, Ugni Blanc, Calitor, Gamay and Camarèse

Gamay

Châtillon-en-Diois AOC

May contain up to 25% Syrah and Pinot Noir

Northern Rhône

KEY

▢ Sweet Fortified

▢ Dry

Rosé Wine Appellations of Alsace, the Loire, Champagne, Jura & Savoie

Pinor Gris	Pinot Noir	Gamay	Cabernet Sauvignon, Cabernet Franc	Cabernet Franc

Reuilly AOC

Central Vineyards

Menetou-Salon AOC

Sancerre AOC

Coteaux de Loir AOC

May also contain Cabernet Franc, Pineau d'Aunis, Malbec

Touraine AOC

May also contain Cabernet Franc, Pineau d'Aunis, Grolleau

Touraine-Amboise AOC

May also contain Gamay, Malbec

Touraine-Mesland AOC

May also contain Gamay, Malbec

Bourgueil AOC

May use up to 10% Cabernet Sauvignon

Chinon AOC

May use up to 10% Cabernet Sauvignon

St.-Nicolas-de-Bourgueil AOC

May use up to 10% Cabernet Sauvignon

Touraine

Poulsard, Trousseau & Pinot Noir

(Vin d') Alsace AOC Pinot Noir

Alsace

Cheverny AOC

At least 50% Gamay; may also use Malbec, Pineau d'Aunis, Pinot Gris

Arbois AOC

Côtes du Jura AOC

Jura

Rosé de Riceys AOC

Coteaux Champenois AOC

May also use Chardonnay and Pinot Meunier

Champagne

Cabernet d'Anjou AOC

Cabernet de Saumur AOC

(Rosé d') Anjou AOC

Mostly Grolleau, with Cabernet Sauvignon, Cabernet Franc, Pineau d'Aunis, Gamay, Malbec

Anjou-Saumur

Touraine Azay-le-Rideau AOC

May also contain Malbec

Gamay, Mondeuse, Pinot Noir & Persan

Vin de Savoie AOC

May also contain Cabernet Sauvignon, Cabernet Franc, Étraire de la Dui, Syrah, Joubertin and up to 20% in total of Aligoté, Altesse, Jacquère, Chardonnay, Mondeuse Blanche, Chasselas, Savagnin, Marsanne, Verdesse

Savoie

Côte Roannaise AOC

Pays Nantais

Rosé de Loire AOC

At least 30% Cabernet Sauvignon, Cabernet Franc; may also include Pineau d'Aunis, Pinot Noir, Gamay, Grolleau

KEY

◼ Medium-Sweet

◼ Medium-Dry

◻ Dry

☐ Bone Dry

Grenache Noir dominated blends

Banyuls AOC

At least 50% Grenache Noir, with Grenache Gris, Grenache Blanc, Macabéo, Tourbat, Muscat Blanc à Petit Grains and Muscat d'Alexandrie, with up to 10% in total of Carignan, Cinsault and Syrah

Banyuls Grand Cru AOC

As Banyuls AOC but with at least 75% Grenache Noir

Maury AOC

At least 75% Grenache Noir, up to 10% Macabéo, and Grenache Gris, Grenache Blanc, Muscat Blanc à Petit Grains, Muscat d'Alexandrie and Tourbat, with up to 10% in total of Carignan, Cinsault, Syrah and Listran Negra

Rivesaltes (Rancio) AOC

May also use Muscat Blanc à Petit Grains, Muscat d'Alexandrie, Grenache Gris, Grenache Blanc, Macabéo, Tourbat, plus up to 10% in total Carignan, Cinsault, Syrah and Palomino

Roussillon

Genache Noir and Mourvèdre blends

Collioure AOC

At least 60% in total of Grenache Noir and Mourvèdre, with at least 25% in total of Carignan, Cinsault and Syrah, and up to 30% Grenache Gris

Muscat varieties

Muscat de Lunel AOC

Uses Muscat Rosé à Petit Grains

Muscat de St.-Jean-de-Minervois AOC

Uses Muscat Rosé à Petit Grains

Muscat de Risevaltes AOC

Uses Muscat Blanc à Petit Grains and Muscat d'Alexandrie

Carignan dominated blends

Côtes du Roussillon AOC

Up to 60% Carignan, with at least 20% Syrah and at least 20% Mourvèdre (no two of these three varieties combined may be more than 90%), up to 30% Macabéo, with Cinsault, Grenache Noir and Lladoner Pelut

Coteaux du Languedoc (village name) AOC

Counoise, Grenache Gris, Terret Noir, Bourboulenc, Carignan Blanc, Clairette, Macabéo, Picpoul, Terret Blanc and Ugni Blanc

Costières de Nîmes AOC

Up to 40% Carignan, with up to 40% Cinsault, at least 25% Grenache Noir, and at least 20% in total of Mourvèdre and Syrah, with up to 10% in total of Clairette, Grenache Blanc, Bourboulenc, Ugni Blanc, Marsanne, Roussane, Macabéo and Vermentino

Minervois AOC

Up to 40% Carignan, with at least 60% in total of Grenache Noir, Lladoner Pelut, Syrah and Mourvèdre, plus Cinsault, Picpoul Noir, Terret Noir and Aspiran Noir

Corbières AOC

At least 40% Carignan (60% in some areas), plus Macabéo and Bourboulenc which together can be no more than the Carignan, with at least 25% (35% in some areas) in total of Grenache Noir, Lladoner Pelut, and Syrah, plus Mourvèdre, Picpoul, Terret and up to 20% Cinsault

Grenache Noir, Lladoner Pelut, Mourvèdre and Syrah blends

St.-Chinian AOC

At least 50% in total of Grenache Noir, Lladoner Pelut, Mourvèdre and Syrah, with up to 40% Carignan and up to 30% Cinsault

Faugères AOC

Up to 30% Carignan, up to 30% Cinsault, at least 20% in total of Grenache Noir and Lladoner Pelut, at least 5% Mourvèdre, and Syrah which together with the Mourvèdre must be at least 15%

Languedoc

KEY

Sweet Fortified

Dry

Rosé Wine Appellations of South-West France

Fer Servadou	Tannat	Cabernet Sauvignon, Cabernet Franc and Merlot	Négrette

Marcillac AOC

At least 90% Fer, blended with Cabernet Franc, Cabernet Sauvignon and Merlot

Gaillac AOC

At least 20% Fer, with at least 20% Duras and Syrah to make minimum 60%, blended with Cabernet Sauvignon, Cabernet Franc, Merlot and Gamay

Tarn & Aveyron

Béarn (-Bellocq) AOC

May also contain Cabernet Franc, Cabernet Sauvignon, Fer, Manseng Noir, Courbu Noir

Irouléguy AOC

Blended with a minimum 50% in total of Cabernet Franc and Cabernet Sauvignon

Pyrénées

Buzet AOC

May also contain Malbec

Côtes du Marmandais AOC

Blended with between 25% and 50% in total of Arbouriou, Malbec, Fer, Gamay and Syrah

Côtes de Duras AOC

May also contain Malbec

Bergerac AOC

May also contain Malbec, Fer and Mérille

Dordogne

Côtes du Frontonnais AOC

Between 50% and 70% Négrette blended with a maximum 25% in total of Malbec, Mérille, Fer, Syrah, Cabernet Sauvignon and Cabernet Franc, and a maximum 15% in total of Gamay, Cinsault and Mauzac

Garonne

KEY

Medium-Dry

Dry

47

Rosé Wine Appellations of Provence & Corsica

Mourvèdre

Bandol AOC

May also contain Grenache Noir and Cinsault, up to 10% Syrah and up to 10% Carignan, although these two must be no more than 15% of the total

Carignan

Côtes de Provence AOC

Up to 40% Carignan, with Cinsault, Grenache Noir, Mourvèdre, Tibouren and up to 30% Syrah, and up to 30% in total of Barbarossa, Cabernet Sauvignon, Calitor, Clairette, Sémillon, Ugni Blanc and Vermentino

Grenache Noir

Palette AOC

At least 50% in total of Grenache Noir, Mourvèdre and Cinsault, with Téoulier, Durif, Muscat (any variety), Carignan, Syrah, Castets, Brun Fourca, Terret Gris, Petit-Brun, Tibouren, Cabernet Sauvignon, and up to 15% in total of Clairette, Picardan, Ugni Blanc, Ugni Rosé, Grenache Blanc, Picpoul, Pascal, Aragnan, Colombard and Terret-Bourret

Cassis AOC

At least 90% in total of Grenache Noir, Mourvèdre, Carignan, Cinsault and Barbarossa, with Terret Noir, Terret Gris, Terret Blanc, Terret Ramenée, Aramon and Aramon Gris

Coteaux Varois AOC

At least 40% Grenache Noir, which together with Mourvèdre and Syrah must be more than 80% of the total, with Cinsault, Carignan, Cabernet Sauvignon and Tibouren

Coteaux d'Aix-en-Provence AOC

At least 60% Grenache Noir, with Cinsault, Counoise, Mourvèdre, Syrah, up to 30% Cabernet Sauvignon, up to 30% Carignan, and up to 10% in total of Bourboulenc, Clairette, Grenache Blanc, Vermentino, Ugni Blanc, Sauvignon Blanc and Sémillon

Les Baux de Provence AOC

At least 60% in total of Grenache Noir, Syrah and Cinsault, with Counoise, Carignan, Cabernet Sauvignon and Mourvèdre

Braquet, Fuella and Cinsault

Bellet AOC

At least 60% in total of Braquet, Fuella and Cinsault, with Grenache Noir, Vermentino, Ugni Blanc, Mayorquin, Clairette, Bourboulenc, Chard-onnay, Pignerol and Muscat à Petits Grains

Sciacarello and Nielluccio

Ajaccio AOC

At least 40% Sciacarello, which together with Barbarossa, Nielluccio and Vermentino must be more than 60% of the total, with a maximum of 40% in total of Grenache Noir, Cinsault, and up to 15% Carignan

Patrimonio AOC

At least 90% Nielluccio, with Grenache Noir, Sciacarello and Vermentino

Vin de Corse (village name) AOC

At least 50% in total of Nielluccio, Sciacarello and Grenache Noir, with Cinsault, Mourvèdre, Barbarossa, Syrah and up to 20% in total of Carignan and Vermentino

Corsica

Provence

KEY

Medium-Dry

Dry

Sparkling Red & Rosé Wine Appellations

Cabernet Franc

Touraine Mousseux
AOC

Touraine Mousseux
AOC

May also contain Malbec, Noble, Gamay and Grolleau

Touraine Pétillant
AOC

Touraine Pétillant
AOC

May also contain Malbec, Noble, Gamay and Grolleau

Crémant de Loire
AOC

May also contain Grolleau Noir, Chenin Blanc, Cabernet Sauvignon, Pineau d'Aunis, Pinot Noir, Chardonnay, Arbois and Grolleau Gris

Saumur Mousseux
AOC

May also contain Cabernet Sauvignon, Malbec, Gamay, Grolleau, Pineau d'Aunis and Pinot Noir

Rosé d'Anjou Pétillant/ Anjou (Rosé) Pétillant AOC

May also contain Grolleau, Cabernet Sauvignon, Pineau d'Aunis, Gamay and Malbec

Anjou Mousseux
AOC

May also contain Cabernet Sauvignon, Malbec, Gamay, Grolleau and Pineau d'Aunis

Loire

Pinot Noir

Crémant de Bourgogne
AOC

May also contain Pinot Gris, Pinot Blanc, Chardonnay, Sacy, Aligoté, Melon de Bourgogne, and up to 20% Gamay

Bourgogne Mousseux
AOC

May also contain Gamay, César and Tressot

Burgundy

Crémant d'Alsace
AOC

Alsace

Duras

Gaillac Mousseux Méthode Gaillaçoise AOC

At least 60% Duras, with Fer, Gamay, Syrah, Cabernet Sauvignon, Cabernet Franc and Merlot

Gaillac Mousseux Méthode Gaillaçoise Doux AOC

As Gaillac Mousseux Méthode Gaillaçoise AOC

South-West France

Chardonnay, Pinot Noir and Pinot Meunier

Champagne
AOC Rosé

Champagne

Cabernet Sauvignon, Cabernet Franc and Merlot

Crémant de Bordeaux
AOC

May also contain Carmenère, Malbec and Petit Verdot

Bordeaux

KEY

■ Sweet Red

□ Dry Red

■ Medium-Sweet Rosé

■ Semi Sweet Rosé

□ Dry Rosé

Sparkling White Wine Appellations of Northern France

Chenin Blanc

Pinot Noir, Pinot Gris, Pinot Blanc and Chardonnay

Chardonnay, Pinot Noir and Pinot Meunier

Pinot Noir and Pinot Meunier

Montlouis Mousseux
AOC

Montlouis Pétillant
AOC

Touraine Mousseux
AOC

May also contain Arbois and up to 20% Chardonnay

Touraine Pétillant
AOC

May also contain Arbois, Sauvignon Blanc and up to 20% Chardonnay

Vouvray Mousseux
AOC

May also contain Arbois

Vouvray Pétillant
AOC

May also contain Arbois

Crémant de Loire
AOC

May also contain Cabernet Franc, Chardonnay, Cabernet Sauvignon, Pineau d'Aunis, Pinot Noir, Arbois, Grolleau Noir and Grolleau Gris

Saumur Mousseux
AOC

May also contain up to 20% in total of Chardonnay and Sauvignon Blanc, and up to 60% in total of Cabernet Sauvignon, Cabernet Franc, Malbec, Gamay, Grolleau, Pineau d'Aunis and Pinot Noir

Anjou Pétillant
AOC

At least 80% Chenin Blanc, with Chardonnay and Sauvignon Blanc

Anjou Mousseux
AOC

At least 60% Chenin Blanc, with Cabernet Sauvignon, Cabernet Franc, Malbec, Gamay, Grolleau and Pineau d'Aunis

Loire

Crémant de Bourgogne
AOC

May also contain Sacy, Aligoté, Melon de Bourgogne, and up to 20% Gamay

Burgundy

Crémant d'Alsace
AOC

May also contain Auxerrois and Riesling

Alsace

Champagne
AOC Brut

Champagne
AOC Demi-Sec

Champagne
AOC Blanc-de-Noirs

Chardonnay

Champagne
AOC Blanc-de-Blancs

Champagne

KEY

☐ Sweet

■ Off-Dry

☐ Dry

☐ Bone Dry

Sparkling White Wine Appellations of Southern France

Altesse

Vin de Savoie Mousseux/ Mousseux de Savoie AOC

May also contain Aligoté, Jacquère, Chardonnay, Pinot Gris, Mondeuse Blanche, Chasselas, Molette, Savagnin, Roussette d'Ayze, Marsanne, Verdesse

Vin de Savoie Pétillant/ Pétillant de Savoie AOC

May also contain Aligoté, Jacquère, Chardonnay, Pinot Gris, Mondeuse Blanche, Chasselas, Savagnin, Roussette d'Ayze, Marsanne, Verdesse

Vin de Savoie Ayze Mousseux AOC

May also contain Savagnin and up to 30% Roussette d'Ayze

Vin de Savoie Ayze Pétillant AOC

May also contain Savagnin and up to 30% Roussette d'Ayze

Savagnin and Chardonnay

Arbois Mousseux AOC

May also contain Pinot Blanc

Côtes du Jura Mousseux AOC

May also contain Pinot Blanc

L'Étoile Mousseux AOC

May also contain Poulsard

Crémant du Jura AOC

May also contain Poulsard or Pinot Blanc

Molette and Chasselas

Seyssel Mousseux AOC

May also contain up to 10% Altesse

Jura & Savoie

Mauzac

Crémant de Limoux AOC

May contain up to 30% in total of Chardonnay and Chenin Blanc, although neither may be more than 20% of the total

Blanquette de Limoux AOC

May contain up to 10% in total of Chardonnay and Chenin Blanc

Blanquette Méthode Ancestrale AOC

Languedoc-Roussillon

Len de l'El and Sauvignon Blanc

Gaillac Mousseux Méthode Gaillaçoise AOC

Must contain more than 15% Len de l'El and more than 15% Sauvignon Blanc, with Mauzac, Mauzac Rosé, Muscadelle, Ondenc and Sémillon

Gaillac Mousseux Méthode Gaillaçoise Doux AOC

As Gaillac Mousseux Méthode Gaillaçoise AOC

South-West France

Clairette

Crémant de Die AOC

Marsanne and Rousanne

St.-Péray Mousseux AOC

Muscat à Petits Grains

Clairette de Die Méthode Dioise Ancestrale AOC

May also contain up to 25% Clairette

Rhône

Sémillon, Sauvignon Blanc and Muscadelle

Crémant de Bordeaux AOC

May also contain Ugni Blanc, Colombard, Cabernet Sauvignon, Cabernet Franc, Carmenère, Merlot, Malbet and Petit Verdot

Bordeaux

KEY

- ☐ Sweet
- ◼ Off-Dry
- ◻ Dry
- ☐ Bone Dry

Section III:
Index of Appellations

Index of Appellations

Index of Appellations

J

Jasnières, Loire, Touraine, white p.37
Juliénas, Burgundy, Beaujolais, red p.15
Jurançon, Gascony, Pyrénées, white p.41
Jurançon Sec, Gascony, Pyrénées, white p.41

K

Klevener de Heiligenstein, Alsace, white p.38

L

L'Etoile, Jura, white p.39
L'Étoile Mousseux, Jura, sparkling white p.51
L'Etoile Vin de Paille, Jura, white p.39
L'Etoile Vin Jeune, Jura, white p.39
L'Hermitage, Rhône, North, red p.23
La Grand Rue Grand Cru, Burgundy, Côtes de Nuits, red p.14
La Romanée Grand Cru, Burgundy, Côtes de Nuits, red p.14
La Tâche Grand Cru, Burgundy, Côtes de Nuits, red p.14
Ladoix (Premier Cru), Burgundy, Côtes de Beaune, red p.14, white p.29
Ladoix Côtes de Beaune, Burgundy, red p.14
Lalande-de-Pomerol, Bordeaux, Libournais, red p.20
Latricères-Chambertin Grand Cru, Burgundy, Côtes de Beaune, red p.14
Le Montrachet Grand Cru, Burgundy, Côtes de Beaune, white p.29
Le Musigny Grand Cru, Burgundy, Côtes de Nuits, white p.29
Les Baux de Provence, red p.28, rosé p.48
Limoux, Languedoc, white p.40

Lirac, Rhône, South, red p.23, white p.36, rosé p.44
Listrac-Médoc, Bordeaux, red p.20
Loupiac, Bordeaux, Entre-Deux-Mers, white p.34
Lussac-St.-Émilion, Bordeaux, Libournais, red p.20

M

Mâcon, Burgundy, Mâconnais, red p.15, white p.29, rosé p.43
Mâcon Supérieur, Burgundy, Mâconnais, red p.15, white p.29, rosé p.43
Mâcon Villages, Burgundy, Mâconnais, white p.29
Madiran, Gascony, Pyrénées, red p.27
Maranges (Premier Cru), Burgundy, Côtes de Beaune, red p.14, white p.29
Maranges Côtes de Beaune, Burgundy, red p.14
Marcillac, Gascony, Tarn & Aveyron, red p.27, rosé p.47
Margaux, Bordeaux, Médoc, red p.20
Marsannay, Burgundy, Côtes de Nuits, red p.14, white p.29, rosé p.43
Marsannay La Côte, Burgundy, Côtes de Nuits, red p.14, white p.29
Maury, Roussillon, red p.26, white p.40, rosé p.46
Mazoyères-Chambertin Grand Cru, Burgundy, Côtes de Nuits, red p.14
Mazis Grand Cru, Burgundy, Côtes de Nuits, red p.14
Mazy-Chambertin Grand Cru, Burgundy, Côtes de Nuits, red p.14
Médoc, Bordeaux, red p.20
Menetou-Salon, Loire, Central Vinyards, red p.24, white p.37, rosé p.45

Mercurey (Premier Cru), Burgundy, Côte Chalonnaise, red p.15, white p.29
Meursault (Premier Cru), Burgundy, Côtes de Beaune, red p.14, white p.29
Meursault-Blagny Premier Cru, Burgundy, Côtes de Beaune, white p.29
Meursault Côtes de Beaune, Burgundy, red p.14
Meursault-Santenots, Burgundy, Côtes de Beaune, red p.14
Minervois, Languedoc, red p.26, white p.40, rosé p.46
Monbazillac, Gascony, Dordogne, white p.41
Montagne-St.-Émilion, Bordeaux, Libournais, red p.20
Montagny (Premier Cru), Burgundy, Côte Chalonnaise, white p.29
Monthelie (Premier Cru), Burgundy, Côtes de Beaune, red p.14, white p.29
Monthelie Côtes de Beaune, Burgundy, red p.14
Montlouis, Loire, Touraine, white p.37
Montlouis Mousseux, Loire, sparkling white p.50
Montlouis Pétillant, Loire, sparkling white p.50
Montrachet Grand Cru, Burgundy, Côtes de Beaune, white p.29
Montravel, Gascony, Dordogne, white p.41
Morey-St.-Denis (Premier Cru), Burgundy, Côtes de Nuits, red p.14, white p.29
Morgon, Burgundy, Beaujolais, red p.15
Moulin-à-Vent, Burgundy, Beaujolais, red p.15
Moulis, Bordeaux, Médoc, red p.20
Moulis-en-Médoc, Bordeaux, red p.20
Mousseux de Savoie, sparkling white p.51
Muscadet, Loire, Pays Nantais, white p.37
Muscadet Coteaux de la Loire, white p.37

Index of Appellations

St.-Émilion Premier Grand Cru Classé, Bordeaux, Libournais, red p.20

St.-Estèphe, Bordeaux, Médoc, red p.20

Ste.-Foy-Bordeaux, red p.20, white p.34

St.-Georges-St.-Émilion, Bordeaux, Libournais, red p.20

St.-Joseph, Rhône, North, red p.23, white p.36

St.-Julien, Bordeaux, Médoc, red p.20

St.-Nicholas-de-Bourgueil, Loire, Touraine, red p.24

St.-Nicolas-de-Bourgueil, Loire, Touraine, rosé p.45

St.-Péray, Rhône, North, white p.36

St.-Péray Mousseux, Rhône, sparkling white p.51

St.-Romain, Burgundy, Côtes de Beaune, red p.14, white p.29

St.-Romain Côtes de Beaune, Burgundy, red p.14

St.-Véran, Burgundy, Mâconnais, white p.29

Sancerre, Loire, Central Vinyards, red p.24, white p.37, rosé p.45

Santenay (Premier Cru), Burgundy, Côtes de Beaune, red p.14, white p.29

Santenay Côtes de Beaune, Burgundy, red p.14

Saumur, Loire, Anjou-Saumur, red p.24, white p.37

Saumur Mousseux, Loire, sparkling rosé p.49, sparkling white p.50

Saumur-Champigny, Loire, Anjou-Saumur, red p.24

Saussignac, Gascony, Dordogne, white p.41

Sauternes, Bordeaux, Graves, white p.34

Savennières, Loire, Anjou-Saumur, white p.37

Savigny (Premier Cru), Burgundy, Côtes de Beaune, red p.14

Savigny Côtes de Beaune, Burgundy, red p.14

Savigny-Lès-Beaune (Premier Cru), Burgundy, Côtes de Beaune, red p.14, white p.29

Savigny-Lès-Beaune Côtes de Beaune, Burgundy, red p.14

Seyssel, Savoie, white p.39

Seyssel Mousseux, Savoie, sparkling white p.51

T

Tâche Grand Cru, Burgundy, Côtes de Nuits, red p.14

Tavel, Rhône, South, rosé p.44

Touraine, Loire, red p.24, white p.37, rosé p.45

Touraine-Amboise, Loire, red p.24, white p.37, rosé p.45

Touraine Azay-le-Rideau, Loire, white p.37, rosé p.45

Touraine-Mesland, Loire, red p.24, white p.37, rosé p.45

Touraine Mousseux, Loire, sparkling red p.49, sparkling rosé p.49, sparkling white p.50

Touraine Pétillant, Loire, sparkling red p.49, sparkling rosé p.49, sparkling white p.50

V

Vacqueyras, Rhône, South, red p.23, white p.36, rosé p.44

Vézelay, Burgundy, Chablis, white p.29

Vin d'Alsace, red p.24, white p.38, rosé p.45

Vin de Bandol, Provence, white p.42

Vin de Bellet, Provence, white p.42

Vin de Corse, Corsica, red p.28, white p.42, rosé p.48

Vin de Frontignan, Languedoc, white p.40

Vin de Paille d'Arbois, Jura, white p.39

Vin de Paille de l' Etoile, Jura, white p.39

Vin de Savoie, red p.25, white p.39, rosé p.45

Vin de Savoie Ayze Mousseux, sparkling white p.51

Vin de Savoie Ayze Pétillant, sparkling white p.51

Vin de Savoie Mousseux, sparkling white p.51

Vin de Savoie Pétillant, sparkling white p.51

Vin Jeune d'Arbois, Jura, white p.39

Vin Jeune de l' Etoile, Jura, white p.39

Viré-Clessé, Burgundy, Mâconnais, white p.29

Volnay (Premier Cru), Burgundy, Côtes de Beaune, red p.14

Volnay-Santenots Premier Cru, Burgundy, Côtes de Beaune, red p.14

Vosne-Romanée (Premier Cru), Burgundy, Côtes de Nuits, red p.14

Vougeot (Premier Cru), Burgundy, Côtes de Nuits, red p.14, white p.29

Vouvray, Loire, Touraine, white p.37

Vouvray Mousseux, Loire, sparkling white p.50

Vouvray Pétillant, Loire, sparkling white p.50

Section IV:
Index of Grape Varieties

Index of Grape Varieties

A

Aligoté, white, grown in Burgundy and Savoie.

Pure varietal form found in CHÂTILLON-EN-DIOIS white.

Primary grape variety in white versions of BOURGOGNE-ALIGOTÉ, BOUZERON, white BEAUJOLAIS, white BEAUJOLAIS SUPÉRIEUR, white BEAUJOLAIS-VILLAGES, white COTEAUX DU LYONNAIS and white BOURGOGNE GRAND-ORDINAIRE.

Secondary blending variety which may be used in BROUILLY red, CRÉMANT DE BOURGOGNE white and rosé, VIN DE SAVOIE MOUSSEUX/MOUSSEUX DE SAVOIE, VIN DE SAVOIE PÉTILLANT/PÉTILLANT DE SAVOIE and VIN DE SAVOIE white and rosé.

Altesse, white, grown in Savoie where it is also known as *Roussette*.

Pure varietal form found in SEYSSEL.

Primary grape variety in white VIN DE SAVOIE, ROUSSETTE DE SAVOIE, VIN DE SAVOIE MOUSSEUX/MOUSSEUX DE SAVOIE, VIN DE SAVOIE PÉTILLANT/PÉTILLANT DE SAVOIE, VIN DE SAVOIE AYZE MOUSSEUX, VIN DE SAVOIE AYZE PÉTILLANT and SEYSSEL MOUSSEUX.

Secondary blending variety which may be used in red and rosé VIN DE SAVOIE,

Aragnan, white, grown in Provence. Secondary blending variety which may be used in all colours of PALETTE.

Aramon, red, grown in Provence. Secondary blending variety which may be used in CASSIS red and rosé.

Aramon Gris, white, grown in Provence. Secondary blending variety which may be used in CASSIS red and rosé.

Arbois, white, grown in the Loire valley. Not to be confused ARBOIS AOC. Secondary blending variety which may be used in CHEVERNY, all colours of CRÉMANT DE LOIRE, and all styles of both TOURAINE and VOUVRAY.

Arbouriou, red, secondary blending variety from South West France which is also known as *Early Burgundy* in California. Secondary blending variety which may be used in CÔTE DU MARMANDAIS.

Arrufiac, white, grown in the Pyrénées. Secondary blending variety which may be used in PACHERENC DU VIC-BILH.

Aspiran, red, grown in the Languedoc. Secondary blending variety which may be used in MINERVOIS red and rosé.

Auxerrois, white, grown in Alsace. Not to be confused with *Malbec*, which is called *Auxerrois* in the Lot *département*.

Pure varietal form found in (VIN D') ALSACE AUXERROIS.

Secondary blending variety which may be used in CRÉMANT D'ALSACE, EDELZWICKER and non-varietal white (VIN D') ALSACE.

B

Barbarossa, red, grown in Corsica, and Provence where it is known locally as Barbaroux. Secondary blending variety which may be used in red and rosé versions of CASSIS, CÔTES DE PROVENCE, AJACCIO and VIN DE CORSE.

Bourboulenc, white, grown in the Southern Rhône, Provence and Languedoc.

Primary grape variety in white CÔTES DU VENTOUX, together with *Clairette*.

Secondary blending variety which may be used in red and rosé CÔTES DU VENTOUX, all colours of CÔTES-DU-RHÔNE, all colours of CÔTES-DU-RHÔNE-VILLAGES, red and white CHÂTEAUNEUF-DU-PAPE, red and rosé GIGONDAS, all colours of COTEAUX DU TRICASTIN, red and rosé RASTEAU, white and rosé CÔTES DU LUBÉRON, white and rosé LIRAC, white VACQUEYRAS, rosé TAVEL, all colours of CORBIÈRES, white MINERVOIS, white and rosé COSTIÈRES DE NÎMES, white and rosé COTEAUX DU LANGUEDOC, all colours of BELLET, white BANDOL and white and rosé COTEAUX D'AIX-EN-PROVENCE.

Braquet, red, grown in Provence. Secondary blending variety which may be used in BELLET.

Brun Fourca, red, grown in Provence. Secondary blending variety which may be used in red or rosé PALETTE.

C

Cabernet Franc, red, grown in Bordeaux, the Loire valley, Savoie and South-West France.

Pure varietal form found in red TOURAINE MOUSSEUX and red TOURAINE PÉTILLANT.

Almost pure varietal form found in red and rosé CHINON (more than 90%), red and rosé BOURGUEIL (more than 90%), red and rosé ST.-NICHOLAS-DE-BOURGUEIL.

Primary grape variety in red Bordeaux (BORDEAUX, BORDEAUX SUPÉRIEUR, MÉDOC, HAUT-MÉDOC, LISTRAC-MÉDOC, MOULIS, MARGAUX, ST.-JULIEN, PAUILLAC, ST.-ESTÈPHE, GRAVES, PESSAC-LÉOGNAN, ST.-ÉMILION,

Index of Grape Varieties

Lussac-St.-Émilion, Montagne-St.-Émilion, Puisseguin-St.-Émilion, St.-Georges-St.-Émilion, Pomerol, Lalande-de-Pomerol, Bordeaux-Côtes-de-Francs, Bordeaux Supérieur Côtes-de-Francs, Côtes-Canon-Fronsac/Canon-Fronsac, Fronsac, Premières Côtes de Bordeaux, Graves de Vayres, Ste.-Foy-Bordeaux, Côtes de Bourg, Premières Côtes de Bourg and Blaye), rosé Bordeaux (Bordeaux, Bordeaux Clairet, Bordeaux Rosé, Bordeaux Supérieur Clairet and Bordeaux Supérieur Rosé), rosé Crémant de Bordeaux, red and rosé Touraine-Amboise, red and rosé Touraine-Mesland, rosé Touraine Mousseux, rosé Touraine Pétillant, Rosé de Loire, Cabernet d'Anjou, Cabernet de Saumur, red Saumur, Saumur-Champigny, Anjou-Villages, red and rosé Anjou, red and rosé Touraine, rosé Crémant de Loire, rosé Saumur Mousseux, Rosé d'Anjou, rosé Anjou Pétillant/Anjou (Rosé) Pétillant, rosé Anjou Mousseux, red and rosé Irouléguy, red and rosé Buzet, red and rosé Côtes du Marmandais, red and rosé Côtes de Duras, red and rosé Bergerac, Côtes de Bergerac, Pécharmant, red and rosé Côtes du Frontonnais

Secondary blending variety that may be used in Cheverny, red and rosé Coteaux de Loir, white Crémant de Loire, white Saumur Mousseux, white Anjou Mousseux, red and rosé Vin de Savoie, red and rosé Béarn, Madiran, red and rosé Marcillac, red and rosé Gaillac, rosé Gaillac Mousseux Méthode Gaillaçoise and rosé Gaillac Mousseux Méthode Gaillaçoise Doux.

Cabernet Sauvignon, red, grown in Bordeaux, the Loire valley, Savoie, Provence and South-West France.

Primary grape variety in red Bordeaux (Bordeaux, Bordeaux Supérieur, Médoc, Haut-Médoc, Listrac-Médoc, Moulis, Margaux, St.-Julien, Pauillac, St.-Estèphe, Graves, Pessac-Léognan, St.-Émilion, Lussac-St.-Émilion, Montagne-St.-Émilion, Puisseguin-St.-Émilion, St.-Georges-St.-Émilion, Pomerol, Lalande-de-Pomerol, Bordeaux-Côtes-de-Francs, Bordeaux Supérieur Côtes-de-Francs, Côtes-Canon-Fronsac/Canon-Fronsac, Fronsac, Premières Côtes de Bordeaux, Graves de Vayres, Ste.-Foy-Bordeaux, Côtes de Bourg, Premières Côtes de Bourg and Blaye), rosé Bordeaux (Bordeaux, Bordeaux Clairet, Bordeaux Rosé, Bordeaux Supérieur Clairet and Bordeaux Supérieur Rosé) and rosé Crémant de Bordeaux.

Secondary blending variety that may be used in Cheverny, red and rosé Touraine, red and rosé Chinon, red and rosé Bourgueil, red and rosé St.-Nicholas-de-Bourgueil, red and rosé Coteaux de Loir, red and rosé Touraine-Amboise, red and rosé Touraine-Mesland, rosé Touraine Mousseux, rosé Touraine Pétillant, white and rosé Crémant de Loire, white and rosé Saumur Mousseux, white and rosé Anjou Mousseux, Rosé de Loire, Cabernet d'Anjou, Cabernet de Saumur, red Saumur, Saumur-Champigny, Anjou-Villages, red and rosé Anjou, red and rosé Irouléguy, red and rosé Buzet, red and rosé Côtes du Marmandais, red and rosé Côtes de Duras, red and rosé Bergerac, Côtes de Bergerac, Pécharmant, red and rosé Côtes du Frontonnais, red and rosé Vin de Savoie, red and rosé Béarn, Madiran, red and rosé Marcillac, red and rosé Gaillac, red and rosé Coteaux d'Aix-en-Provence, red and rosé Coteaux Varois, red and rosé Côtes de Provence, red and rosé Les Baux de Provence and red and rosé Palette.

Calitor, red, grown in Provence and the Southern Rhône. Secondary blending variety which may be used in red or rosé Côtes de Provence, and all colours of Côtes-du-Rhône, Côtes-du-Rhône-Villages, Rasteau, Tavel and Gigondas.

Camaralet, white, grown in the Pyrénées. Secondary blending variety which may be used in white Béarn and Jurançon.

Camarèse, red, grown in the Southern Rhône. Secondary blending variety which may be used in red or rosé Vacqueyras, and all colours of Côtes-du-Rhône, Côtes-du-Rhône-Villages, Gigondas and Rasteau.

Carignan Blanc, white, grown in the Languedoc. Secondary blending variety which may be used in white or rosé Coteaux du Languedoc.

Carignan, red, grown in Southern Rhône, Provence, Corsica and Languedoc-Roussillon.

Primary grape variety in red and rosé Côtes du Ventoux (up to 30%), red and rosé Côtes de Lubéron (up to 20%), red Gigondas (up to 20%), red and rosé Coteaux du Tricastin (up to 20%), red and rosé Côtes du Roussillon (up to 60%), Fitou (up to 75%), red and rosé Minervois (up to 40%), red and rosé Costières de Nîmes (up to 40%), red and rosé Corbières (at least 40%), red and rosé St.-Chinian (up to 40%), red and rosé Faugères (up to 30%), red and rosé Bandol (up to 10%), red and rosé Ajaccio (up to 15), red and rosé Coteaux d'Aix-en-Provence (up to 30%), red and rosé Côtes de Provence (up to 40%), white and rosé Côtes-du-Rhône (up to 30%), red and rosé Banyuls, red and rosé Banyuls Grand Cru, red and rosé Rivesaltes, all colours of Maury and rosé Tavel (up to 10%),

Secondary blending variety which may be used in Coteaux de Pierrevert, all colours of Côtes-du-Rhône-Villages, red and rosé Lirac, red and rosé

COTEAUX DU LANGUEDOC, red and rosé VIN DE CORSE, red and rosé CASSIS, red and rosé COTEAUX VAROIS, red and rosé LES BAUX DE PROVENCE, red and rosé PALETTE, white and rosé RASTEAU and red and rosé COLLIOURE.

Carmenère, red, grown in Bordeaux. Secondary blending variety which may be used in all red and rosé generic Bordeaux (BORDEAUX, BORDEAUX SUPÉRIEUR, BORDEAUX CLAIRET, BORDEAUX ROSÉ, BORDEAUX SUPÉRIEUR CLAIRET, BORDEAUX SUPÉRIEUR ROSÉ), all wines of the Médoc (MÉDOC, HAUT-MÉDOC, LISTRAC-MÉDOC, MOULIS, MARGAUX, ST.-JULIEN, PAUILLAC and ST.-ESTÈPHE), CÔTES-DE-CASTILLON, ST.-ÉMILION, LUSSAC-ST.-ÉMILION, PUISSEGUIN-ST.-ÉMILION, red PESSAC-LÉOGNAN, all red wines of Entre-Deux-Mers (PREMIÈRES CÔTES DE BORDEAUX, GRAVES DE VAYRES and STE.-FOY-BORDEAUX), and all colours of CRÉMANT DE BORDEAUX.

Castets, red, grown in Provence. Secondary blending variety which may be used in red or rosé PALETTE.

César, red, grown in Burgundy. Secondary blending variety which may be used in red or rosé BOURGOGNE, rosé BOURGOGNE GRAND-ORDINAIRE and BOURGOGNE MOUSSEUX. + Irancy

Chardonnay, white, grown in Burgundy, the Loire, Jura, Provence, Languedoc-Roussillon, .

Pure varietal form found in CHABLIS, CHABLIS GRAND CRU, PETIT CHABLIS, white MARSANNAY, white MUSIGNY, white ALOXE-CORTON, CHARLEMAGNE, white CORTON, CORTON-CHARLEMAGNE, MONTRACHET, CRIOTS-BÂTARD-MONTRACHET, BÂTARD-MONTRACHET, CHEVALIER-MONTRACHET, BIENVENUES-BÂTARD-MONTRACHET, POUILLY-FUISSÉ, POUILLY-LOCHÉ, POUILLY-VINZELLES, ST.-VÉRAN, CHÂTILLON-EN-DIOIS

CHARDONNAY and CHAMPAGNE BLANC-DE-BLANCS.

Primary grape variety in white BOURGOGNE, white BOURGOGNE HAUTES-CÔTES DE NUITS, white CÔTES NUITS-VILLAGES, white FIXIN, white MOREY-ST.-DENIS, white NUITS, white VOUGEOT, VÉZELAY, white GIVRY, white MERCUREY, MONTAGNY, white RULLY, white AUXEY-DURESSES, white BEAUNE, white BOURGOGNE HAUTE-CÔTES DE BEAUNE, white CHOREY-LÈS-BEAUNE, white CHASSAGNE-MONTRACHET, white PULIGNY-MONTRACHET, white CÔTES DE BEAUNE, white LADOIX, white MARANGES, white MEURSAULT, MEURSAULT-BLAGNY, white MONTHELIE, white PERNAND-VERGELESSES, white ST.-AUBIN, white ST.-ROMAIN, white SANTENAY, white SAVIGNY-LÈS-BEAUNE, white MÂCON, white MÂCON SUPÉRIEUR, MÂCON VILLAGES, VIRÉ-CLESSÉ, white ARBOIS, ARBOIS-PUPILLIN, VIN JEUNE D'ARBOIS/ARBOIS VIN JEUNE, CHÂTEAU-CHALON, CÔTES DU JURA, CÔTES DU JURA VIN JEUNE, L'ETOILE, VIN DE PAILLE DE L' ETOILE/ L'ETOILE VIN DE PAILLE, VIN DE PAILLE D'ARBOIS/ARBOIS VIN DE PAILLE, CÔTES DU JURA VIN DE PAILLE, LIMOUX, white and rosé CRÉMANT DE BOURGOGNE.

Secondary blending variety which may be used in red BOURGOGNE PASSETOUTGRAINS, red BROUILLY, all colours of COTEAUX CHAMPENOIS, red and rosé VIN DE SAVOIE, BOURGOGNE-ALIGOTÉ, BOUZERON, white BEAUJOLAIS, white BEAUJOLAIS SUPÉRIEUR, white BEAUJOLAIS-VILLAGES, white COTEAUX DU LYONNAIS and white BOURGOGNE GRAND-ORDINAIRE, white SAUMUR, white ANJOU, white TOURAINE, white CHEVERNY, white BELLET, white and rosé CRÉMANT DE LOIRE, white SAUMUR MOUSSEUX, white ANJOU PÉTILLANT, white TOURAINE MOUSSEUX, white TOURAINE PÉTILLANT, white CRÉMANT D'ALSACE and white and rosé CHAMPAGNE.

Chasselas, white, grown in the Loire valley, Alsace and Jura. Also known as *Fendant* in Switzerland.

Pure varietal form found in CRÉPY, VIN DE SAVOIE MARIGNAN, VIN DE SAVOIE RIPAILLE, (VIN D') ALSACE CHASSELAS.

Primary grape variety in POUILLY-SUR-LOIRE.

Secondary blending variety which may be used in EDELZWICKER, non-varietal white (VIN D') ALSACE, VIN DE SAVOIE MOUSSEUX/MOUSSEUX DE SAVOIE, VIN DE SAVOIE PÉTILLANT/PÉTILLANT DE SAVOIE, SEYSSEL MOUSSEUX and all colours of VIN DE SAVOIE.

Chenin Blanc, white, primarily grown in the Loire valley, but also grown in Blaye, Bourg, Languedoc-Roussillon and the Dordogne. Also known as *Steen* in South Africa.

Pure varietal form found in SAVENNIÈRES, ANJOU COTEAUX DE LA LOIRE, COTEAUX DE L'AUBANCE, COTEAUX DE SAUMUR, BONNEZEAUX, COTEAUX DU LAYON, COTEAUX DU LAYON-CHAUME, COTEAUX DU LAYON VILLAGES, white COTEAUX DE LOIR, white TOURAINE-AMBOISE, white CHINON, white TOURAINE-MESLAND, TOURAINE AZAY-LE-RIDEAU, JASNIÈRES, MONTLOUIS, MONTLOUIS MOUSSEUX, MONTLOUIS PÉTILLANT and QUARTS-DE-CHAUME.

Primary grape variety in white SAUMUR, SAUMUR MOUSSEUX, white ANJOU, ANJOU PÉTILLANT, ANJOU MOUSSEUX, VOUVRAY, VOUVRAY MOUSSEUX, VOUVRAY PÉTILLANT, TOURAINE MOUSSEUX, TOURAINE PÉTILLANT and white CRÉMANT DE LOIRE.

Secondary blending variety which may be used in white BLAYE, white CÔTES DE BLAYE, white CÔTES DE BOURG, white TOURAINE, white CHEVERNY, LIMOUX,

Index of Grape Varieties

RIVESALTES, SAUSSIGNAC, white BERGERAC, white CÔTES DE DURAS, rosé CRÉMANT DE LOIRE, CRÉMANT DE LIMOUX, BLANQUETTE DE LIMOUX.

Cinsault, red, widely planted in the Southern Rhône, Languedoc-Roussillon, Provence, Corsica and the Garonne. Secondary blending variety which may be used in Southern Rhône reds and rosés (CHÂTEAUNEUF-DU-PAPE, CÔTES-DU-RHÔNE, CÔTES-DU-RHÔNE-VILLAGES, GIGONDAS, LIRAC, COTEAUX DU TRICASTIN, RASTEAU, CÔTE DU VENTOUX, COTEAUX DE PIERREVERT, CÔTE DE LUBÉRON, VACQUEYRAS), Roussillon reds and rosés (BANYULS, BANYULS GRAND CRU, RIVESALTES, COLLIOURE, CÔTES DU ROUSSILLON, CÔTES DU ROUSSILLON VILLAGES and FITOU), red and rosé COSTIÈRES DE NÎMES, red and rosé MINERVOIS, red and rosé CORBIÈRES, ST.-CHINIAN, COTEAUX DU LANGUEDOC, FAUGÈRES, CÔTES DU FRONTONNAIS, BANDOL, red COTEAUX D'AIX-EN-PROVENCE, red AJACCIO, red VIN DE CORSE and rosé CASSIS.

Clairette, white, grown in Southern Rhône, Provence and Languedoc-Roussillon.

Pure varietal form found in COTEAUX DE DIE, CRÉMANT DE DIE, CLAIRETTE DE BELLEGARDE and CLAIRETTE DU LANGUEDOC.

Primary grape variety in CLAIRETTE DE DIE MÉTHODE DIOISE ANCESTRALE (up to 25%).

Secondary blending variety which may be used in all colours of CÔTES DU VENTOUX, all colours of CÔTES-DU-RHÔNE, all colours of CÔTES-DU-RHÔNE-VILLAGES, red CHÂTEAUNEUF-DU-PAPE, red and rosé GIGONDAS, all colours of COTEAUX DU TRICASTIN, white and rosé RASTEAU, white and rosé CÔTES DU LUBÉRON, white and rosé LIRAC, white VACQUEYRAS, all colours of CÔTES DE PROVENCE, all colours of

PALETTE, all colours of BELLET, white CORBIÈRES, white and rosé COSTIÈRES DE NÎMES, white and rosé COTEAUX DU LANGUEDOC, white and rosé COTEAUX D'AIX-EN-PROVENCE, white BANDOL, white CASSIS, white COTEAUX VARIOS and rosé TAVEL.

Colombard, white, grown in Bordeaux and Provence. Secondary blending variety which may be used in white BORDEAUX, white BORDEAUX SUPÉRIEUR, white CRÉMANT DE BORDEAUX, white CÔTES DE BOURG, white BLAYE, white CÔTES DE BLAYE, ENTRE-DEUX-MERS, ENTRE-DEUX-MERS-HAUT-BENAUGE, white STE.-FOY-BORDEAUX, white GRAVES DE VAYRES and all colours of PALETTE.

Counoise, red, grown primarily in the Southern Rhône, but also in Languedoc-Roussillon and Provence. Adds a peppery flavour to blends. Secondary blending variety which may be used in all colours of CHÂTEAUNEUF-DU-PAPE, all colours of CÔTES-DU-RHÔNE, red CÔTES-DU-RHÔNE-VILLAGES, all colours of GIGONDAS, red and rosé RASTEAU, red and rosé CÔTES DU VENTOUX, red and rosé CÔTES DU LUBÉRON, red and rosé VACQUEYRAS, red and rosé COTEAUX DU LANGUEDOC, red and rosé COTEAUX D'AIX-EN-PROVENCE and all colours of LES BAUX DE PROVENCE.

Courbu Noir, red, grown in the Pyrénées. Secondary blending variety which may be used in red or rosé BÉARN.

D

Duras, red, grown in the Tarn *département* in South-West France. Secondary blending variety which may be used in red or rosé GAILLAC, GAILLAC MOUSSEUX MÉTHODE GAILLAÇOISE, GAILLAC MOUSSEUX MÉTHODE GAILLAÇOISE DOUX.

Durif, red, grown in Provence. Secondary blending variety which may be used in red or rosé PALETTE.

E

Étraire de la Dui, red, grown in Savoie. Secondary blending variety which may be used in red or rosé VIN DE SAVOIE.

F

Fer (Servadou), red, grown in South-West France.

Primary grape variety in MARCILLAC (more than 90%), and red and rosé GAILLAC (more than 20%).

Secondary blending variety which may be used in red BÉARN, MADIRAN, red and rosé CÔTES DU MARMANDAIS, red and rosé CÔTES DU FRONTONNAIS, red and rosé BERGERAC, CÔTES DE BERGERAC, GAILLAC MOUSSEUX MÉTHODE GAILLAÇOISE and GAILLAC MOUSSEUX MÉTHODE GAILLAÇOISE DOUX.

Folle Blanche, white. Secondary blending variety which may be used in white BLAYE and CÔTES DE BLAYE.

Fuella, red, grown in Provence. Secondary blending variety which may be used in BELLET.

G

Gamay, red, grown in Burgundy, the Rhône valley, the Loire valley, Savoie and South-West France.

Pure varietal form found in CHIROUBLES, COTEAUX DU LYONNAIS, RÉGNIÉ, FLEURIE, JULIÉNAS, ST.-AMOUR, CHÉNAS, Morgon, MOULIN-À-VENT, ANJOU GAMAY and VIN DE SAVOIE GAMAY.

Primary grape variety in red and rosé BOURGOGNE PASSETOUTGRAINS, rosé BOURGOGNE GRAND-ORDINAIRE, red and rosé BEAUJOLAIS, red and rosé

BEAUJOLAIS SUPÉRIEUR, red and rosé BEAUJOLAIS-VILLAGES, BROUILLY, CÔTES DE BROUILLY, red and rosé MÂCON, red and rosé MÂCON SUPÉRIEUR, red and rosé CHÂTILLON-EN-DIOIS, red and rosé CHEVERNY, red and rosé TOURAINE, rosé TOURAINE AZAY-LE-RIDEAU, rosé COTEAUX DE LOIR, non-varietal red and rosé VIN DE SAVOIE.

Secondary blending variety which may be used in red BOURGOGNE, white and rosé CRÉMANT DE BOURGOGNE, red CÔTES DE LUBÉRON, red and rosé VACQUEYRAS, red and rosé GIGONDAS, all colours of CÔTES-DU-RHÔNE, all colours of CÔTES-DU-RHÔNE-VILLAGES, all colours of RASTEAU, red COTEAUX DE LOIR, red and rosé TOURAINE-AMBOISE, red and rosé TOURAINE-MESLAND, rosé GAILLAC MOUSSEUX MÉTHODE GAILLAÇOISE, rosé and white SAUMUR MOUSSEUX, white ANJOU MOUSSEUX, red and rosé GAILLAC, red and rosé CÔTES DU MARMANDAIS and red and rosé CÔTES DU FRONTONNAIS.

Gewürztraminer, white, grown in Alsace.

Pure varietal form found in (VIN D') ALSACE GEWÜRZTRAMINER, ALSACE GRAND CRU GEWÜRZTRAMINER, ALSACE GEWÜRZTRAMINER VENDAGE TARDIVES, ALSACE GRAND CRU GEWÜRZTRAMINER VENDAGE TARDIVES, ALSACE GEWÜRZTRAMINER SÉLECTION DE GRAINS NOBLES and ALSACE GRAND CRU GEWÜRZTRAMINER SÉLECTION DE GRAINS NOBLES.

Primary grape variety in non-varietal white (VIN D') ALSACE and EDELZWICKER.

Grenache (Noir), red, grown in the Southern Rhône, Provence and Languedoc-Roussillon.

Primary grape variety in all colours of red and rosé CÔTES DE LUBÉRON, red and rosé VACQUEYRAS, red and rosé CÔTES-DU-RHÔNE-VILLAGES, red and

rosé GIGONDAS, red and rosé LIRAC, red and rosé COTEAUX D'AIX-EN-PROVENCE, red and rosé CASSIS, red and rosé COTEAUX VAROIS, red and rosé LES BAUX DE PROVENCE, red and rosé COLLIOURE, all colours of MAURY, all colours of BANYULS and all colours of BANYULS GRAND CRU.

Secondary blending variety which may be used in red and rosé CÔTES-DU-RHÔNE, red and rosé CHÂTEAUNEUF-DU-PAPE, red and rosé COTEAUX DU TRICASTIN, red COTEAUX DE PIERREVERT, red and rosé CÔTES DU VENTOUX, TAVEL, red and rosé ST.-CHINIAN, red and rosé COTEAUX DU LANGUEDOC, red and rosé FAUGÈRES, red and rosé AJACCIO, red and rosé PATRIMONIO, red and rosé VIN DE CORSE, red PALETTE, red and rosé BELLET, red and rosé COSTIÈRES DE NÎMES, red and rosé CORBIÈRES, all colours of RIVESALTES, red and rosé CÔTES DU ROUSSILLON, red and rosé BANDOL and red and rosé CÔTES DE PROVENCE.

Grenache Blanc, white, grown in the Southern Rhône, Provence and Languedoc-Roussillon.

Primary grape variety in all colours of RASTEAU, white COTEAUX DU TRICASTIN, white CÔTES DU LUBÉRON, white CÔTES-DU-RHÔNE, white CHÂTEAUNEUF-DU-PAPE, white LIRAC, white VACQUEYRAS, white CORBIÈRES and white MINERVOIS.

Secondary blending variety which may be used in all colours of CÔTES DU VENTOUX, red and rosé COTEAUX DU TRICASTIN, rosé CÔTES DU LUBÉRON, rosé LIRAC, red and white BANYULS, red and white BANYULS GRAND CRU, all colours of MAURY, all colours of RIVESALTES, all colours of PALETTE, white CÔTES-DU-RHÔNE-VILLAGES, white and rosé COSTIÈRES DE NÎMES, white COTEAUX DU LANGUEDOC,

white and rosé COTEAUX D'AIX-EN-PROVENCE and white COTEAUX VARIOS.

Grenache Gris, white, grown in Languedoc-Roussillon and the Southern Rhône. Secondary blending variety which may be used in red and rosé BANYULS, red and rosé BANYULS GRAND CRU, all colours of RIVESALTES, all colours of MAURY, red and rosé COTEAUX DU LANGUEDOC, all colours of RASTEAU and rosé COLLIOURE.

J

Jacquère, white, grown in Savoie. Secondary blending variety which may be used in all colours of VIN DE SAVOIE, VIN DE SAVOIE MOUSSEUX/MOUSSEUX DE SAVOIE and VIN DE SAVOIE PÉTILLANT/PÉTILLANT DE SAVOIE.

Joubertin, red, grown in Savoie. Secondary blending variety which may be used in red and rosé VIN DE SAVOIE.

Jurançon Noir, red, grown in the Lot *département*. Not to be confused with JURANÇON (SEC) AOC. Secondary blending variety which may be used in CAHORS.

L

Lauzet, white, grown in the Pyrénées. Secondary blending variety which may be used in white BÉARN and JURANÇON.

Len de l'El, white, grown in South-West France.

Primary grape variety in non-varietal white GAILLAC MOUSSEUX MÉTHODE GAILLAÇOISE (more than 15%) and GAILLAC MOUSSEUX MÉTHODE GAILLAÇOISE DOUX (more than 15%).

Index of Grape Varieties

Secondary blending variety which may be used in white GAILLAC, GAILLAC DOUX and GAILLAC PREMIER CÔTES.

Listran Negra, red, grown in Roussillon. Secondary blending variety which may be used in all colours of MAURY.

Lladoner Pelut, red, grown in Languedoc-Roussillon. Secondary blending variety which may be used in red or rosé CÔTES DU ROUSSILLON, CÔTES DU ROUSSILLON VILLAGES, FITOU, red or rosé MINERVOIS, red or rosé CORBIÈRES, ST.-CHINIAN, red COTEAUX DU LANGUEDOC and FAUGÈRES.

M

Macabéo, white, grown in Languedoc-Roussillon.

Primary grape variety in white CÔTES DU ROUSSILLON, together with Tourbat.

Secondary blending variety which may be used in all colours of BANYULS and BANYULS GRAND CRU, all colours of RIVESALTES, all colours of MAURY, red or rosé CÔTES DU ROUSSILLON, FITOU, all colours of CORBIÈRES, white MINERVOIS, LIMOUX, white or rosé COSTIÈRES DE NÎMES, white or rosé COTEAUX DU LANGUEDOC.

Malbec, red, grown in Bordeaux, South-West France and the Loire.

Primary grape variety in CAHORS (more than 70%).

Secondary blending variety which may be used in red Bordeaux (BORDEAUX, BORDEAUX SUPÉRIEUR, MÉDOC, HAUT-MÉDOC, LISTRAC-MÉDOC, MOULIS, MARGAUX, ST.-JULIEN, PAUILLAC, ST.-ESTÈPHE, GRAVES, PESSAC-LÉOGNAN, ST.-ÉMILION, LUSSAC-ST.-ÉMILION, MONTAGNE-ST.-ÉMILION, PUISSEGUIN-ST.-ÉMILION, ST.-

GEORGES-ST.-ÉMILION, POMEROL, LALANDE-DE-POMEROL, BORDEAUX-CÔTES-DE-FRANCS, BORDEAUX SUPÉRIEUR CÔTES-DE-FRANCS, CÔTES-CANON-FRONSAC/CANON-FRONSAC, FRONSAC, PREMIÈRES CÔTES DE BORDEAUX, GRAVES DE VAYRES, STE.-FOY-BORDEAUX, CÔTES DE BOURG, PREMIÈRES CÔTES DE BOURG and BLAYE), rosé Bordeaux (BORDEAUX, BORDEAUX CLAIRET, BORDEAUX ROSÉ, BORDEAUX SUPÉRIEUR CLAIRET and BORDEAUX SUPÉRIEUR ROSÉ), rosé CRÉMANT DE BORDEAUX, red and rosé CHEVERNY, red TOURAINE, red and rosé TOURAINE-AMBOISE, red and rosé TOURAINE-MESLAND, rosé TOURAINE AZAY-LE-RIDEAU, rosé TOURAINE MOUSSEUX, rosé TOURAINE PÉTILLANT, ROSÉ D'ANJOU, rosé COTEAUX DE LOIR, white and rosé SAUMUR MOUSSEUX, white and rosé ANJOU MOUSSEUX, ROSÉ D'ANJOU PÉTILLANT/ANJOU (ROSÉ) PÉTILLANT, red and rosé BUZET, red and rosé CÔTES DU MARMANDAIS, red and rosé CÔTES DU FRONTONNAIS, red and rosé CÔTES DE DURAS, red and rosé BERGERAC, CÔTES DE BERGERAC and PÉCHARMANT.

Manseng Noir, red, grown in the Pyrénées. Secondary blending variety which may be used in red and rosé BÉARN.

Marsanne, white, grown in the Rhône, Languedoc-Roussillon, Provence and Savoie.

Primary grape variety (together with *Roussanne*) in white ST.-JOSEPH, ST.-PÉRAY, white ST.-PÉRAY MOUSSEUX, white CROZES-HERMITAGE, white HERMITAGE, HERMITAGE VIN DE PAILLE. *Rousanne* dominated wines tend to be finer, and *Marsanne* dominated wines tend to be richer.

Secondary blending variety which may be used in red ST.-JOSEPH, red CROZES-HERMITAGE, red HERMITAGE, red and rosé CÔTES-DU-RHÔNE-VILLAGES, red and rosé GIGONDAS, BRÉZÈME-CÔTES-DU-RHÔNE,

all colours of RASTEAU, white COTEAUX DU TRICASTIN, white and rosé CÔTES DU LUBÉRON, white and rosé LIRAC, white VACQUEYRAS, white and rosé CÔTES-DU-RHÔNE, white MINERVOIS, white and rosé COSTIÈRES DE NÎMES, white COTEAUX DU LANGUEDOC, white CASSIS, all colours of VIN DE SAVOIE, VIN DE SAVOIE MOUSSEUX/MOUSSEUX DE SAVOIE and VIN DE SAVOIE PÉTILLANT/PÉTILLANT DE SAVOIE.

Mauzac, see *Malbec*.

Mauzac Rosé, pink, grown in South-West France. Secondary blending variety which may be used in GAILLAC MOUSSEUX MÉTHODE GAILLAÇOISE and GAILLAC MOUSSEUX MÉTHODE GAILLAÇOISE DOUX.

Mayorquin, white, grown in the Provence. Secondary blending variety which may be used in all colours of BELLET.

Melon de Bourgogne, white, grown in Burgundy and the Loire valley.

Pure varietal form found in MUSCADET, MUSCADET COTEAUX DE LA LOIRE, MUSCADET CÔTES DE GRANDLIEU and MUSCADET DE SÈVRE-ET-MAINE.

Secondary blending variety which may be used in red BROUILLY, white VÉZELAY, white BOURGOGNE GRAND-ORDINAIRE and white and rosé CRÉMANT DE BOURGOGNE.

Mérille, red, grown in South-West France. Secondary blending variety which may be used in CÔTES DU FRONTONNAIS, red or rosé BERGERAC and CÔTES DE BERGERAC.

Merlot, red, grown in Bordeaux and South-West France.

Primary grape variety in red Bordeaux (BORDEAUX, BORDEAUX SUPÉRIEUR, MÉDOC, HAUT-MÉDOC, LISTRAC-MÉDOC, MOULIS, MARGAUX, ST.-JULIEN, PAUILLAC, ST.-

ESTÈPHE, GRAVES, PESSAC-LÉOGNAN, ST.-ÉMILION, LUSSAC-ST.-ÉMILION, MONTAGNE-ST.-ÉMILION, PUISSEGUIN-ST.-ÉMILION, ST.-GEORGES-ST.-ÉMILION, POMEROL, LALANDE-DE-POMEROL, BORDEAUX-CÔTES-DE-FRANCS, BORDEUAX SUPÉRIEUR CÔTES-DE-FRANCS, CÔTES-CANON-FRONSAC/CANON-FRONSAC, FRONSAC, PREMIÈRES CÔTES DE BORDEAUX, GRAVES DE VAYRES, STE.-FOY-BORDEAUX, CÔTES DE BOURG, PREMIÈRES CÔTES DE BOURG and BLAYE), rosé Bordeaux (BORDEAUX, BORDEAUX CLAIRET, BORDEAUX ROSÉ, BORDEAUX SUPÉRIEUR CLAIRET and BORDEAUX SUPÉRIEUR ROSÉ) and white and rosé CRÉMANT DE BORDEAUX.

Secondary blending variety which may be used in red and rosé GAILLAC, GAILLAC MOUSSEUX MÉTHODE GAILLAÇOISE, GAILLAC MOUSSEUX MÉTHODE GAILLAÇOISE DOUX, red and rosé MARCILLAC, CAHORS, red and rosé BUZET, red and rosé CÔTES DU MARMANDAIS, red and rosé CÔTES DE DURAS, red and rosé BERGERAC, CÔTES DE BERGERAC and PÉCHARMANT.

Merlot Blanc, white, grown in Bordeaux. Secondary blending variety which may be used in some of the white wines of Bordeaux: BORDEAUX (up to 30%), BORDEAUX SUPÉRIEUR (up to 15%), ENTRE-DEUX-MERS (up to 30%), ENTRE-DEUX-MERS-HAUT-BENAUGE (up to 30%), STE.-FOY-BORDEAUX (up to 10%), GRAVES DE VAYRES (up to 30%), BLAYE, CÔTES DE BLAYE and CÔTES DE BOURG.

Molette, white, grown in Savoie.

Primary grape variety in SEYSSEL MOUSSEUX, together with Chasselas.

Secondary blending variety which may be used in VIN DE SAVOIE MOUSSEUX/MOUSSEUX DE SAVOIE and VIN DE SAVOIE PÉTILLANT/PÉTILLANT DE SAVOIE.

Mondeuse, red, grown in Savoie.

Pure varietal form found in VIN DE SAVOIE MONDEUSE.

Secondary blending variety which may be used in red and rosé VIN DE SAVOIE.

Mondeuse Blanche, white, grown in Savoie. Secondary blending variety which may be used in ROUSSETTE DE SAVOIE, all colours of VIN DE SAVOIE, VIN DE SAVOIE MOUSSEUX/MOUSSEUX DE SAVOIE and VIN DE SAVOIE PÉTILLANT/PÉTILLANT DE SAVOIE.

Muscadelle, white, grown in Bordeaux and South-West France. Secondary blending variety which may be used in all white wines of Bordeaux (BORDEAUX, BORDEAUX SUPÉRIEUR, GRAVES, GRAVES SUPÉRIEUR, PESSAC-LÉOGNAN, CÉRONS, BARSAC, SAUTERNES, ENTRE-DEUX-MERS, ENTRE-DEUX-MERS-HAUT-BENAUGE, STE.-FOY-BORDEAUX, GRAVES DE VAYRES, BORDEAUX HAUT-BENAUGE, PREMIÈRES-CÔTES-DE-BORDEAUX, CADILLAC, CÔTES DE BORDEAUX-ST.-MACAIRE, LOUPIAC, ST.-CROIX-DU-MONT, BORDEAUX-CÔTES-DE-FRANCS, BORDEAUX-CÔTES-DE-FRANCS LIQUOREUX, CÔTES DE BOURG, BLAYE, CÔTES DE BLAYE and PREMIÈRES CÔTES DE BLAYE), white wines of the Dordogne (BERGERAC, SAUSSIGNAC, MONTRAVEL, HAUT-MONTRAVEL, CÔTES DE MONTRAVEL, MONBAZILLAC and ROSETTE), BUZET, CÔTES DE DURAS, GAILLAC PREMIER CÔTES and GAILLAC.

Muscardin, red, grown in the Southern Rhône. Secondary blending variety which may be used in all colours of CÔTES-DU-RHÔNE, red CÔTES-DU-RHÔNE-VILLAGES, red and rosé GIGONDAS, red and rosé RASTEAU, red and rosé VACQUEYRAS and red and white CHÂTEAUNEUF-DU-PAPE.

Muscat à Petit Grains, multiple synonym for *Muscat Blanc à Petit Grains* or *Muscat Rosé à Petit Grains*.

Muscat d'Alsace, see *Muscat à Petit Grains*.

Muscat d'Alexandrie, white, grown in Languedoc-Roussillon.

Primary grape variety in white and rosé MUSCAT DE RISEVALTES.

Secondary blending variety which may be used in all colours of BANYULS, all colours of BANYULS GRAND CRU, all colours of RIVESALTES and all colours of MAURY.

Muscat Blanc à Petit Grains, white, grown in Alsace, Provence, Corsica and Languedoc-Roussillon.

Pure varietal form found in white MUSCAT DE BEAUMES-DE-VENISE, MUSCAT DU CAP CORSE, MUSCAT DE FRONTIGNAN/ VIN DE FRONTIGNAN, white MUSCAT DE LUNEL, MUSCAT DE MIREVAL, white MUSCAT DE ST.-JEAN-DE-MINERVOIS,

Primary grape variety in white and rosé MUSCAT DE RISEVALTES.

Optional Muscat variety used in varietal Alsace Muscats (ALSACE MUSCAT, ALSACE GRAND CRU MUSCAT, ALSACE MUSCAT VENDAGE TARDIVES, ALSACE GRAND CRU MUSCAT VENDAGE TARDIVES, ALSACE MUSCAT SÉLECTION DE GRAINS NOBLES, ALSACE GRAND CRU MUSCAT SÉLECTION DE GRAINS NOBLES).

Optional Muscat variety used for primary blending in non-varietal white (VIN D') ALSACE and EDELZWICKER.

Index of Grape Varieties

Secondary blending variety which may be used in all colours of BANYULS, all colours of BANYULS GRAND CRU, all colours of RIVESALTES, all colours of MAURY, white CORBIÈRES, white BELLET and white MINERVOIS.

Muscat Rosé à Petit Grains, pink, grown in Alsace, Provence and Languedoc-Roussillon.

Pure varietal form found in rosé MUSCAT DE BEAUMES-DE-VENISE, rosé MUSCAT DE LUNEL and rosé MUSCAT DE ST.-JEAN-DE-MINERVOIS,

Optional Muscat variety used in varietal Alsace Muscats (ALSACE MUSCAT, ALSACE GRAND CRU MUSCAT, ALSACE MUSCAT VENDAGE TARDIVES, ALSACE GRAND CRU MUSCAT VENDAGE TARDIVES, ALSACE MUSCAT SÉLECTION DE GRAINS NOBLES, ALSACE GRAND CRU MUSCAT SÉLECTION DE GRAINS NOBLES).

Optional Muscat variety used for primary blending in non-varietal white (VIN D') ALSACE and EDELZWICKER.

Secondary blending variety which may be used in white BELLET and white MINERVOIS.

Muscat Ottonel, white, grown in Alsace.

Optional Muscat variety used in varietal Alsace Muscats (ALSACE MUSCAT, ALSACE GRAND CRU MUSCAT, ALSACE MUSCAT VENDAGE TARDIVES, ALSACE GRAND CRU MUSCAT VENDAGE TARDIVES, ALSACE MUSCAT SÉLECTION DE GRAINS NOBLES, ALSACE GRAND CRU MUSCAT SÉLECTION DE GRAINS NOBLES).

Optional Muscat variety used for primary blending in non-varietal white (VIN D') ALSACE and EDELZWICKER.

N

Négrette, red, grown in the Garonne département in South-West France.

Primary grape variety in red and rosé CÔTES DU FRONTONNAIS (50-70%).

Nielluccio, red, grown in Corsica.

Primary grape variety in red and rosé PATRIMONIO (more than 90%).

Secondary blending variety which may be used in red and rosé AJACCIO and VIN DE CORSE.

O

Ondenc, white, grown in Bordeaux and South-West France. Secondary blending variety which may be used in white BORDEAUX, white GAILLAC, GAILLAC PREMIER CÔTES, GAILLAC MOUSSEUX MÉTHODE GAILLAÇOISE, GAILLAC MOUSSEUX MÉTHODE GAILLAÇOISE Doux, MONTRAVEL, white BERGERAC and white CÔTES DE DURAS.

P

Palomino, white, grown in Roussillon. Secondary blending variety which may be used in all colours of RIVESALTES.

Pascal Blanc, white, grown in the Southern Rhône and Provence. Secondary blending variety which may be used in red CÔTES DU VENTOUX, all colours of CÔTES-DU-RHÔNE, all colours of CÔTES-DU-RHÔNE-VILLAGES, red and rosé GIGONDAS, all colours of RASTEAU, white COTEAUX D'AIX-EN-PROVENCE, white CASSIS, white CÔTES DE PROVENCE.

Petit-Brun, red, grown in Provence. Secondary blending variety which may be used in red and rosé PALETTE.

Persan, red, grown in Savoie. Secondary blending variety which may be used is red and rosé VIN DE SAVOIE.

Petit Verdot, red, grown in Bordeaux. Secondary blending variety which may be used in red and rosé generic Bordeaux (BORDEAUX, BORDEAUX SUPÉRIEUR, BORDEAUX CLAIRET, BORDEAUX ROSÉ, BORDEAUX SUPÉRIEUR CLAIRET, BORDEAUX SUPÉRIEUR ROSÉ), all wines of the Médoc (MÉDOC, HAUT-MÉDOC, LISTRAC-MÉDOC, MOULIS, MARGAUX, ST.-JULIEN, PAUILLAC and ST.-ESTÈPHE), CÔTES-DE-CASTILLON, red PESSAC-LÉOGNAN, red GRAVES, red BLAYE and white and rosé CRÉMANT DE BORDEAUX.

Picpoul (Blanc), white, grown in the Rhône. Secondary blending variety which may be used in red CÔTES DU VENTOUX, red CÔTES DE LUBÉRON, all colours of CÔTES-DU-RHÔNE, red and rosé CÔTES-DU-RHÔNE-VILLAGES, red and rosé GIGONDAS, TAVEL, all colours of RASTEAU, all colours of CORBIÈRES, white MINERVOIS, white and rosé COTEAUX DU LANGUEDOC, all colours of PALETTE, white COTEAUX DU TRICASTIN, white and rosé LIRAC and white CHÂTEAUNEUF-DU-PAPE.

Picpoul Noir, red, grown in the Rhône and the Languedoc. Secondary blending variety which may be used in red CHÂTEAUNEUF-DU-PAPE, red and rosé CÔTES DU VENTOUX, red and rosé COTEAUX DU TRICASTIN, red and rosé MINERVOIS and red COTEAUX DU LANGUEDOC.

Pignerol, pink, grown in Provence. Secondary blending variety which may be used in all colours of BELLET.

Index of Grape Varieties

NUITS, rosé MARSANNAY and rosé BOURGOGNE HAUTE-CÔTES DE BEAUNE.

Pinot Meunier, red, grown in Champagne and the Loire. Secondary blending variety which may be used in red TOURAINE, all colours of COTEAUX CHAMPENOIS, white and rosé CHAMPAGNE, and CHAMPAGNE BLANC-DE-NOIRS.

Pinot Noir, red, grown in Burgundy, the Rhône valley, the Loire valley, Jura and Savoie.

Pure varietal form found in red and rosé MENETOU-SALON, red and rosé SANCERRE, red and rosé (VIN D') ALSACE and ROSÉ DE RICEYS.

Primary grape variety in red Burgundy (BOURGOGNE, BOURGOGNE GRAND-ORDINAIRE, BOURGOGNE PASSETOUTGRAINS, GIVRY, RULLY, MERCUREY, ALOXE-CORTON, CORTON, AUXEY-DURESSES, BEAUNE, BLAGNY, CHASSAGNE-MONTRACHET, LADOIX, MARANGES, MONTHELIE, PERNAND-VERGELESSES, POMMARD, PULIGNY-MONTRACHET, ST.-AUBIN, SANTENAY, SAVIGNY, VOLNAY, MEURSAULT, VOLNAY-SANTENOTS, MEURSAULT-SANTENOTS, BOURGOGNE HAUTE-CÔTES DE BEAUNE, CÔTES DE BEAUNE, CÔTES DE BEAUNE-VILLAGES, CHOREY-LÈS-BEAUNE, ST.-ROMAIN, ECHÉZEAUX, GRAND ECHÉZEAUX, VOSNE-ROMANÉE, ROMANÉE-ST.-VIVANT, LA GRAND RUE, RICHEBOURG, LA ROMANÉE, ROMANÉE-CONTI, LA TÂCHE, VOUGEOT, CLOS VOUGEOT, CHAMBOLLE-MUSIGNY, BONNES MARES, MUSIGNY, MOREY-ST.-DENIS, CLOS DU LAMBRAYS, CLOS DE LA ROCHE, CLOS ST.-DENIS, CLOS DE TART, GEVREY-CHAMBERTIN, CHAPELLE-CHAMBERTIN, CHAMBERTIN-CLOS DE BÉZE, CHARMES-CHAMBERTIN, MAZOYÈRES-CHAMBERTIN, MAZY-CHAMBERTIN/MAZIS, RUCHOTTES-CHAMBERTIN, CHAMBERTIN, GRIOTTES-CHAMBERTIN, LATRICÈRES-CHAMBERTIN, NUITS, FIXIN, MARSANNAY, BOURGOGNE HAUTES-CÔTES DE NUITS, CÔTES NUITS-VILLAGES), rosé BOURGOGNE, rosé BOURGOGNE

PASSETOUTGRAINS, rosé BOURGOGNE HAUTES-CÔTES DE NUITS, rosé MARSANNAY, rosé BOURGOGNE HAUTE-CÔTES DE BEAUNE, rosé BOURGOGNE GRAND-ORDINAIRE, white and rosé CRÉMANT DE BOURGOGNE, BOURGOGNE MOUSSEUX, red REUILLY, CHAMPAGNE, CHAMPAGNE ROSÉ, CHAMPAGNE BLANC-DE-NOIRS, all colours of COTEAUX CHAMPENOIS, red CÔTES DU JURA, red ARBOIS, white (VIN D') ALSACE, EDELZWICKER and CRÉMANT D'ALSACE.

Secondary blending variety which may be used in red and rosé BEAUJOLAIS, red and rosé BEAUJOLAIS SUPÉRIEUR, red and rosé BEAUJOLAIS-VILLAGES, CÔTES DE BROUILLY, red and rosé MÂCON, red and rosé MÂCON SUPÉRIEUR, red and rosé CHÂTILLON-EN-DIOIS, red CÔTES DU LUBÉRON, red CHEVERNY, red COTEAUX DE LOIR, red TOURAINE, rosé ROSÉ DE LOIRE, RED VIN DE SAVOIE, (VIN D') ALSACE PINOT/CLEVNER/KLEVNER, white and rosé CRÉMANT DE LOIRE, white and rosé SAUMUR MOUSSEUX.

Poulsard, pink, grown in Jura.

Pure varietal form found in red CÔTES DU JURA POULSARD and red ARBOIS POULSARD.

Primary grape variety in non-varietal red and rosé CÔTES DU JURA and non-varietal red and rosé ARBOIS, VIN DE PAILLE D'ARBOIS/ARBOIS VIN DE PAILLE, CÔTES DU JURA VIN DE PAILLE, VIN DE PAILLE DE L' ETOILE/L'ETOILE VIN DE PAILLE, L'ETOILE, L'ÉTOILE MOUSSEUX and CRÉMANT DU JURA.

Prolongeau, red, grown in Blaye. Secondary blending variety which may be used in BLAYE.

R

Raffiat, white, grown in the Pyrénées. Secondary blending variety which may be used in white BÉARN.

Riesling, white, grown in Alsace.

Pure varietal form found in (VIN D') ALSACE RIESLING, ALSACE GRAND CRU RIESLING, ALSACE RIESLING VENDAGE TARDIVES, ALSACE GRAND CRU RIESLING VENDAGE TARDIVES, ALSACE RIESLING SÉLECTION DE GRAINS NOBLES and ALSACE GRAND CRU RIESLING SÉLECTION DE GRAINS NOBLES.

Primary grape variety in CRÉMANT D'ALSACE, non-varietal white (VIN D') ALSACE and EDELZWICKER.

Rolle, see *Vermentino*.

Romordantin, white, grown in the Loire.

Pure varietal form form only in COUR-CHEVERNY.

Roussanne, white, grown in the Rhône, Languedoc-Roussillon and Savoie.

Pure varietal form form only in VIN DE SAVOIE BERGERON and VIN DE SAVOIE CHIGNIN-BERGERON,

Primary grape variety (together with *Roussanne*) in white ST.-JOSEPH, ST.-PÉRAY, white ST.-PÉRAY MOUSSEUX, white CROZES-HERMITAGE, white HERMITAGE, HERMITAGE VIN DE PAILLE. *Rousanne* dominated wines tend to be finer, and *Marsanne* dominated wines tend to be richer.

Secondary blending variety which may be used in red ST.-JOSEPH, red CROZES-HERMITAGE, red HERMITAGE, all colours of CÔTES DU VENTOUX, all colours of CÔTES-DU-RHÔNE, all colours of CÔTES-DU-RHÔNE-VILLAGES, red and white CHÂTEAUNEUF-DU-PAPE, red and rosé GIGONDAS, BRÉZÈME-CÔTES-DU-RHÔNE, all colours of RASTEAU, white COTEAUX DU TRICASTIN, white and rosé CÔTES DU LUBÉRON, white and rosé LIRAC, white VACQUEYRAS, white

Corbières, white MINERVOIS, white and rosé COSTIÈRES DE NÎMES and white COTEAUX DU LANGUEDOC.

Roussette, synonym for *Altesse* used in Savoie.

Roussette d'Ayze, white, grown in Savoie. Secondary blending variety which may be used in white VIN DE SAVOIE MOUSSEUX/MOUSSEUX DE SAVOIE, VIN DE SAVOIE PÉTILLANT/PÉTILLANT DE SAVOIE, VIN DE SAVOIE AYZE MOUSSEUX (up to 30%) and VIN DE SAVOIE AYZE PÉTILLANT (up to 30%).

S

Sacy, white, grown in Burgundy. Secondary blending variety which may be used in white BOURGOGNE GRAND-ORDINAIRE and white and rosé CRÉMANT DE BOURGOGNE.

Sauvignon Blanc, white, grown in Bordeaux, the Loire, Provence and South-West France.

Pure varietal form found in white MENETOU-SALON, QUINCY, white REUILLY, white SANCERRE, POUILLY-FUMÉ and COTEAUX DU GIENNOIS.

Primary grape variety in white wines of Bordeaux (BORDEAUX, BORDEAUX SUPÉRIEUR, GRAVES, GRAVES SUPÉRIEUR, PESSAC-LÉOGNAN, CÉRONS, BARSAC, SAUTERNES, ENTRE-DEUX-MERS, ENTRE-DEUX-MERS-HAUT-BENAUGE, STE.-FOY-BORDEAUX, GRAVES DE VAYRES, BORDEAUX HAUT-BENAUGE, PREMIÈRES-CÔTES-DE-BORDEAUX, CADILLAC, CÔTES DE BORDEAUX-ST.-MACAIRE, LOUPIAC, ST.-CROIX-DU-MONT, BORDEAUX-CÔTES-DE-FRANCS, BORDEAUX-CÔTES-DE-FRANCS LIQUOREUX, CÔTES DE BOURG, BLAYE, CÔTES DE BLAYE and PREMIÈRES CÔTES DE BLAYE), white TOURAINE, white CHEVERNY, MONTRAVEL, white CÔTES DU MARMANDAIS, white BERGERAC, SAUSSIGNAC, white CÔTES DE DURAS, GAILLAC, GAILLAC PREMIER CÔTES,

white GAILLAC MOUSSEUX MÉTHODE GAILLAÇOISE, white GAILLAC MOUSSEUX MÉTHODE GAILLAÇOISE DOUX, HAUT-MONTRAVEL, CÔTES DE MONTRAVEL, MONBAZILLAC, ROSETTE and white BUZET.

Secondary blending variety which may be used in white SAUMUR, white SAUMUR MOUSSEUX, white ANJOU, white ANJOU PÉTILLANT, POUILLY-SUR-LOIRE, white BÉARN, PACHERENC DU VIC-BILH, white BANDOL, white and rosé COTEAUX D'AIX-EN-PROVENCE, white CASSIS and white TOURAINE PÉTILLANT.

Savagnin, white, grown in Jura and Savoie.

Pure varietal form found in VIN JEUNE DE L' ETOILE/L'ETOILE VIN JEUNE.

Primary grape variety in white ARBOIS, ARBOIS-PUPILLIN, VIN JEUNE D'ARBOIS/ARBOIS VIN JEUNE, ARBOIS MOUSSEUX, CHÂTEAU-CHALON, CÔTES DU JURA, CÔTES DU JURA VIN JEUNE, CÔTES DU JURA MOUSSEUX, L'ETOILE, VIN DE PAILLE DE L' ETOILE/ L'ETOILE VIN DE PAILLE, L'ÉTOILE MOUSSEUX, VIN DE PAILLE D'ARBOIS/ARBOIS VIN DE PAILLE, CÔTES DU JURA VIN DE PAILLE and CRÉMANT DU JURA.

Secondary blending variety which may be used in all colours of non-varietal VIN DE SAVOIE., VIN DE SAVOIE MOUSSEUX/MOUSSEUX DE SAVOIE, VIN DE SAVOIE PÉTILLANT/PÉTILLANT DE SAVOIE, VIN DE SAVOIE AYZE MOUSSEUX and VIN DE SAVOIE AYZE PÉTILLANT.

Savagnin Rosé, pink, grown in Alsace.

Pure varietal form found in KLEVENER DE HEILIGENSTEIN.

Sciacarello, red, grown in Corsica.

Primary grape variety in red and rosé AJACCIO

(between 40% and 60%).

Secondary blending variety which may be used in red and rosé PATRIMONIO and VIN DE CORSE.

Sémillon, white, grown in Bordeaux, South-West France and Provence.

Primary grape variety in white wines of Bordeaux (BORDEAUX, BORDEAUX SUPÉRIEUR, GRAVES, GRAVES SUPÉRIEUR, PESSAC-LÉOGNAN, CÉRONS, BARSAC, SAUTERNES, ENTRE-DEUX-MERS, ENTRE-DEUX-MERS-HAUT-BENAUGE, STE.-FOY-BORDEAUX, GRAVES DE VAYRES, BORDEAUX HAUT-BENAUGE, PREMIÈRES-CÔTES-DE-BORDEAUX, CADILLAC, CÔTES DE BORDEAUX-ST.-MACAIRE, LOUPIAC, ST.-CROIX-DU-MONT, BORDEAUX-CÔTES-DE-FRANCS, BORDEAUX-CÔTES-DE-FRANCS LIQUOREUX, CÔTES DE BOURG, BLAYE, CÔTES DE BLAYE and PREMIÈRES CÔTES DE BLAYE), white Crémant de Bordeaux, white BERGERAC, SAUSSIGNAC, white CÔTES DE DURAS, GAILLAC, GAILLAC PREMIER CÔTES, white GAILLAC MOUSSEUX MÉTHODE GAILLAÇOISE, white GAILLAC MOUSSEUX MÉTHODE GAILLAÇOISE DOUX, HAUT-MONTRAVEL, CÔTES DE MONTRAVEL, MONBAZILLAC, ROSETTE and white BUZET

Secondary blending variety which may be used in red and rosé CÔTES DE PROVENCE, PACHERENC DU VIC-BILH, MONTRAVEL, white CÔTES DU MARMANDAIS, white BELLET and rosé COTEAUX D'AIX-EN-PROVENCE.

Servanin, red, grown in Savoie. Secondary blending variety which may be used in red VIN DE SAVOIE.

Sylvaner, white, grown in Alsace.

Pure varietal form found in (VIN D') ALSACE SYLVANER.

Index of Grape Varieties

Secondary blending variety which may be used in non-varietal white (VIN D') ALSACE and EDELZWICKER.

Syrah, red, grown in the Rhône, Languedoc-Roussillon, South-West France, Savoie, Corsica and Provence.

Pure varietal form found in CORNAS.

Primary grape variety in red ST.-JOSEPH, CÔTE RÔTIE, red CROZES-HERMITAGE, red HERMITAGE, BRÉZÈME-CÔTES-DU-RHÔNE.

Secondary blending variety which may be used in red and rosé CHÂTILLON-EN-DIOIS, red and rosé CÔTES DE LUBÉRON, all colours of CÔTES-DU-RHÔNE, red CÔTES-DU-RHÔNE-VILLAGES, red and white CHÂTEAUNEUF-DU-PAPE, red and rosé COTEAUX DU TRICASTIN, red COTEAUX DE PIERREVERT, TAVEL, red and rosé CÔTES DU VENTOUX, red VACQUEYRAS, red and rosé LIRAC, red GIGONDAS, red and rosé ST.-CHINIAN, red COTEAUX DU LANGUEDOC, all colours of MAURY, red and rosé FAUGÈRES, red and rosé GAILLAC, red GAILLAC MOUSSEAUX MÉTHODE GAILLAÇOISE, rosé GAILLAC MOUSSEAUX MÉTHODE GAILLAÇOISE DOUX, red and rosé CÔTES DU MARMANDAIS, red and rosé CÔTES DU FRONTONNAIS, red and rosé BANDOL, red and rosé VIN DE CORSE, red and rosé COTEAUX D'AIX-EN-PROVENCE, red and rosé COTEAUX VAROIS, red and rosé CÔTES DE PROVENCE, red and rosé LES BAUX DE PROVENCE, red and rosé PALETTE, rosé VIN DE SAVOIE, red and rosé BANYULS, red and rosé BANYULS GRAND CRU, all colours of RIVESALTES, red and rosé COLLIOURE, red and rosé CÔTES DU ROUSSILLON, FITOU, red and rosé COSTIÈRES DE NÎMES, red and rosé MINERVOIS, red and rosé CORBIÈRES.

T

Tannat, red, grown in the Pyrénées.

Primary grape variety in red and rosé BÉARN (at least 60%) and MADIRAN (at least 40%).

Secondary blending variety which may be used in red and rosé IROULÉGUY (up to 50%) and CAHORS.

Téoulier, red, grown in Provence. Secondary blending grape variety which may be used in red and rosé PALETTE.

Terret Blanc, white, grown in Provence and Languedoc. Secondary blending grape variety which may be used in red and rosé CASSIS and white and rosé COTEAUX DU LANGUEDOC.

Terret Gris, white, grown in Provence. Secondary blending grape variety which may be used in red and rosé CASSIS and red and rosé PALETTE.

Terret Noir, red, grown in the Southern Rhône, Languedoc-Roussillon and Provence. Secondary blending grape variety which may be used in all colours of CÔTES-DU-RHÔNE, red and rosé CÔTES-DU-RHÔNE-VILLAGES, red COTEAUX DE PIERREVERT, red and rosé VACQUEYRAS, red and white CHÂTEAUNEUF-DU-PAPE, red and rosé GIGONDAS, red and rosé RASTEAU, FITOU, red and rosé MINERVOIS, red and rosé COTEAUX DU LANGUEDOC and red and rosé CASSIS.

Terret-Bourret, pink, grown in Provence. Secondary blending grape variety which may be used in all colours of PALETTE.

Tibouren, pink, grown in Provence. Secondary blending grape variety which may be used in red and rosé CÔTES DE PROVENCE, red and rosé PALETTE, and rosé COTEAUX VARIOS.

Tourbat, white, grown in Roussillon. Secondary blending grape variety which may be used in all colours of BANYULS, all colours of BANYULS GRAND CRU, all colours of RIVESALTES, all colours of MAURY, and white CÔTES DU ROUSSILLON.

Tressot, see *Trousseau*.

Trousseau, red, grown in Jura. Also known as *Tressot* in Burgundy.

Pure varietal form found in red and rosé CÔTES DU JURA TROUSSEAU, red and rosé ARBOIS TROUSSEAU.

Primary grape variety in non-varietal red and rosé CÔTES DU JURA, non-varietal red and rosé ARBOIS, VIN DE PAILLE D'ARBOIS/ARBOIS VIN DE PAILLE and CÔTES DU JURA VIN DE PAILLE.

Secondary blending variety which may be used in red and rosé BOURGOGNE, rosé BOURGOGNE GRAND-ORDINAIRE and red BOURGOGNE MOUSSEUX.

U

Ugni Blanc, white, grown in the Southern Rhône, Provence, Languedoc-Roussillon, South-West France and Bordeaux. Also known as *Trebbiano* in Italy.

Primary grape variety (together with *Vermentino*) in white AJACCIO, white PATRIMONIO and white VIN DE CORSE.

Secondary blending variety which may be used in red CÔTES DU VENTOUX, all colours of COTEAUX DU TRICASTIN, white and rosé CÔTES DU LUBÉRON, white and rosé LIRAC, all colours of CÔTES-DU-RHÔNE, all colours of CÔTES-DU-RHÔNE-VILLAGES, rosé GIGONDAS, all colours of RASTEAU, all colours of CÔTES DE PROVENCE, all colours of PALETTE, all colours of BELLET, white BORDEAUX, white BLAYE, CÔTES DE BLAYE, white CRÉMANT DE BORDEAUX, all colours of RIVESALTES, white and rosé COSTIÉRES DE NÎMES, white and rosé COTEAUX DU LANGUEDOC, white MONTRAVEL, white BERGERAC, white CÔTES DE DURAS, white CÔTES DU MARMANDAIS, white and rosé COTEAUX D'AIX-EN-PROVENCE, white BANDOL, white CASSIS and white COTEAUX VARIOS.

Ugni Rosé, pink, grown in Provence. Secondary blending variety which may be used in all colours of PALETTE.

V

Vaccarèse, red, grown in the Southern Rhône. Secondary blending grape variety which may be used in red and rosé CÔTES-DU-RHÔNE, all colours of CÔTES-DU-RHÔNE-VILLAGES, red and rosé VACQUEYRAS, red and white CHÂTEAUNEUF-DU-PAPE, red and rosé GIGONDAS, and red and rosé RASTEAU.

Verdesse, white, grown in the Savoie. Secondary blending grape variety which may be used in all colours of non-varietal VIN DE SAVOIE, VIN DE SAVOIE MOUSSEUX/MOUSSEUX DE SAVOIE and VIN DE SAVOIE PÉTILLANT/PÉTILLANT DE SAVOIE.

Vermentino, white, grown in Corsica, Provence, Languedoc and the Southern Rhône. May be known as *Rolle* outside Corsica.

Primary grape variety in all colours of AJACCIO, white PATRIMONIO and white VIN DE CORSE.

Secondary blending variety which may be used in red and rosé PATRIMONIO, red and rosé VIN DE CORSE, white and rosé COTEAUX D'AIX-EN-PROVENCE, all colours of CÔTES DE PROVENCE, all colours of BELLET, white and rosé CÔTES DU LUBÉRON, white CORBIÈRES, white MINERVOIS, white and rosé

COSTIÉRES DE NÎMES and white COTEAUX DU LANGUEDOC.

Viognier, white, grown in the Rhône.

Pure varietal form found in CONDRIEU and CHÂTEAU GRILLET.

Primary grape variety in CÔTE RÔTIE, all colours of CÔTES-DU-RHÔNE, red and white CÔTES-DU-RHÔNE-VILLAGES, red and rosé GIGONDAS, all colours of RASTEAU, white COTEAUX DU TRICASTIN, white and rosé LIRAC and white VACQUEYRAS.